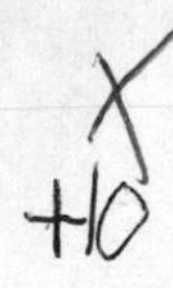

Looking at Central Lancashire

40p.

Uniform with this volume:

Looking at NORTH LANCASHIRE

Looking at SOUTH LANCASHIRE

Other Dalesman books on Lancashire:

ARNSIDE AND SILVERDALE

BOWLAND AND PENDLE HILL

THE CIVIL WAR IN LANCASHIRE

CLITHEROE AND THE RIBBLE VALLEY

GRANGE AND CARTMEL

LANCASHIRE RECIPES

UNDERGROUND IN FURNESS

Looking at
Central Lancashire

by
"Spartina"

THE DALESMAN PUBLISHING COMPANY LTD.
Clapham, (Via Lancaster)
Yorkshire

15BN: 0 85206 108 0

First Published 1971

Printed by Galava Printing Co., Ltd.. Hallam Road, Nelson, Lancs.

Contents

"Spartina" is a group of four Lancashire authors, Dorothy Pilling, Mollie Thompson, Daphne Tibbitt and Diana Underwood. They would like to thank all those persons who have so willingly supplied information and without whose help this book would not have been possible. The front cover photograph of Stoneyhurst College is by Pye's Photo Service of Clitheroe, and the map on the back cover is by Janet Ellerington. Illustrations in the text are by H. Pilling.

Introduction

IN these books, which we hope will be of as much interest to the resident as the visitor, we have tried to dispel the myth that Lancashire is the ugly sister of the North, dull and uninteresting. We hope you will be interested to read of ghosts and witches, the legends associated with them, and the fine abbeys, churches and mansions with which Lancashire abounds. Delve into the past at one of the many museums and examine unique collections of dolls, aircraft and railway engines; try some of the county dishes and see where they are made; or take part in some of the more unusual sports and hobbies or local customs. Take a lazy trip down one of the many canals, search for the wild life or go fishing. Explore the docks and harbours and watch the fishing fleet sail out to sea, following a channel taken by the Vikings many years ago. Lancashire holds many treasures, old and new. It is a county which gives a little of everything—sea and mountain, cities and small hamlets, and each has a place to explore.

1: A Short History of Lancashire

LANCASHIRE and its peoples have lived through many changes from the invasion of the Romans to the invasion of the Industrial Revolution. The county accepted each new influx of men and ideas and absorbed them into its pattern, and it is this pattern which can be rediscovered today in "Looking at Lancashire."

Roman conquest of Britain began in 43 A.D. and it was sixteen years later that the conquest of the North West began, the Romans crossing the Mersey at Latchford and proceeding across the Ribble. The tribe of Brigantes lived in Northern England and they were used by the Roman soldiers to build roads and the garrisons at Ribchester (Brenetennacum) and Manchester (Mancunium). Excavations have revealed a considerable number of Roman objects: inscribed altar stones, coins, jewelry and pottery. A bronze helmet was found at Ribchester in 1796, a bronze bust of Minerva at Warrington and the remains of an altar at Wigan.

When the Angles came into Lancashire from Yorkshire, Northumberland and Durham in about 570 A.D., some settled in the valleys of the Lune and Ribble until the 11th century. The population of Angles increased, names such as Wigan, Treales and Makerfield date back to this period. There have been a few Anglo-Saxon finds; coins at Little Crosby near Liverpool and at Heaton Moor near Lancaster. A chest containing ingots of silver and 10,000 silver coins was found at Cuerdale, near Preston in 1840, and was known as the "Cuerdale Hoard". Some of these coins were Danish and some were of the period of Alfred the Great and his son, Edward the Elder. The Danish invasion of Lancashire began with isolated raids, but evidence of settlement is shown in such names as Hulme, Davyhulme, Levenshulme, Oldham, Flixton and Urmston in the Manchester area. About 900 Norsemen settled in the county and the names Scales, Scarisbrick and Norbreck are Norse, while those of Goosnargh and Grimsargh are of half Irish-Norse descent. Norse crosses have been found at Whalley, Lancaster, Bolton, Winwick, Halton and Urswick. They consist of a circle between the arms of the cross, and are usually of stone and carved with snake and chain decorations. Norse tombs, known as hogsbacks, are to be found at Heysham and Bolton-le-Sands. Edward the Elder and

Aethelflaed, children of Alfred the Great, built forts at Thelwall and Runcorn, while the land between the Ribble and the Mersey was a royal domain until after the Norman Conquest. The Domesday Book states that at this time Lancashire was wooded, with scattered farmsteads and vast areas of rough grassland.

During the reign of William I, the county was administered by the King's cousin, Roger of Poitou, who chose Lancaster as the site for his castle. This was the beginning of Lancashire's close connection with the Royal family. In the 15th century the confiscated lands of the supporters of Lambert Simnel, pretender to the throne, were given to Lord Strange, son of the Earl of Derby. These gifts included estates in Wigan, Bury, Salford and Manchester, estates south of the Ribble and the Broughton estates in Furness and Cartmel, and thus the Derby family became the richest and most important in Lancashire. The Earldom of Derby has played a prominent part in the county throughout the centuries, King Henry VIII and Queen Elizabeth I having stayed at Knowsley Hall, home of the Earls of Derby.

In the reign of Elizabeth I, Lancashire was the strongest Catholic county, although Manchester and Bolton were strongholds of Puritanism. Religious belief was the deciding factor in the Civil War; in 1642 Lord Derby led the Royalists and some years later Cromwell marched down the Ribble valley and gained control of Preston. Later Lord Derby's army was defeated and he was taken prisoner, tried and executed in 1651. During Jacobite times there was dissension and plotting, the Lancashire Jacobites encouraging the Scottish Jacobites to invade England by way of Lancashire. This they did in 1715, but were defeated. The next attempt was in 1745 when Bonnie Prince Charlie with his troops came to Lancaster, Preston and Manchester, planning to march to London, but at Derby he abandoned the march and returned to Preston. In Tudor and Stuart times the population of Lancashire was small, but there were great industrial developments. By the 18th century more people were coming into the county, and with the Industrial Revolution the problem of poverty was rife. It was during this time that Lancashire's cotton industry came to the fore and her trade steadily increased. Mills, coal mines, factories and docks covered large areas. The opening of the Manchester Ship Canal in 1894, the construction of the East Lancashire road in the 1920s and the making of the Mersey Tunnel in 1934 greatly improved communications.

Lancashire with its industrial regions is one of the mainsprings of Britain's commerce. Manchester is the centre of the cotton industry and electrical engineering. St. Helens, largest producer of glass in the world, also has large chemical factories, copper foundries and cable works. Liverpool is one of the world's great trading centres with its docks, shipyards and airport.

2: Traditional Foods

THERE is an old Lancashire saying: "Trouble is naught, cost is all." The inhabitants of the county suffered hardship and poverty during the Industrial Revolution, and this was probably the reason for the traditional foods of Lancashire being cheap, appetising, nourishing, easily prepared and easily obtained. Most families, if fortunate enough to be in employment, were working in the mills, factories and local coal mines, and would buy food on the way home from work. The corner shop and small home-made bakeries were the source of many traditional foods.

Blackburn Fig or Fag Pie.

This is a Mothering Sunday delicacy similar to Bury Simnel Cake in tradition, but unlike the rich fruit cake in other respects. It is a short pastry tart filled with stewed figs, spices, currants and treacle—very sweet and filling. The same pie is used as a traditional Palm Sunday delicacy in the Midlands.

Blackpool Rock.

Blackpool rock comes in a variety of flavours, including mint, pineapple, orange and lime and their corresponding colours. Although now made in almost all seaside resorts, Blackpool proudly claims to have produced the first stick of rock.

Black Puddings.

Black puddings have been made by the Thompson family of Bury since 1865. They are still popular and are sold hot and cold on Bury Market, orders being sent to many parts of Britain. The intestines of a cow are used to make a bag to hold the mixture which consists of pig's blood, groats and small pieces of bacon fat. Cheap and tasty, it is easily cooked by boiling for ten minutes. An old saying in Bury is "Keep it daık, it's a black pudding." In June 1970 H.R.H. Princess Anne saw her first black pudding at a Royal Highland Show and enquired about this delicacy and a selection was accordingly sent to the palace, Public interest was so aroused that extra supplies had to be ordered.

Bolton Hot Pot

Bolton Hot Pot is similar to the traditional Lancashire Hot Pot, but a little more elaborate as it has kidneys, mushrooms and oysters added to the basic recipe. Lancashire Hot Pot is a simple nourishing dish consisting of layers of potatoes and onions with cheap cuts of mutton, stewed slowly in an earthenware dish in the oven. Bolton has added the extra ingredients making a more expensive and richly flavoured stew; perhaps there was more money in Bolton or they wished to improve on the traditional dish. Both hot pots are served with pickled red cabbage.

Bury Simnel Cake.

This is a flat spiced cake, thickest in the centre, containing currants and almonds and having the top baked with sugar and flaked almonds. Its origins are uncertain, but there are at least four different stories:— 1. The name is derived from the fine wheaten flour, "Siminells." 2. It is named after Lambert Simnel, claimant to the throne of Henry VII, Simnel's father being a baker. 3. A couple, Simon and Nell, kept a baker's shop and disagreed about the best way to bake a cake, so to settle their quarrel they decided to use the best of both methods and produced a Simnel Cake—a joint version of their names. 4. Another story is that servant girls in wealthy homes were allowed to return home on one day each year. The mistress would give the girls ingredients to make a cake to take to their mothers; this was eaten on the 4th Sunday in Lent—"Mothering Sunday."

Chorley Cakes.

Chorley Cakes are very popular in Lancashire, They are made from two rounds of short pastry filled with currants, sugar and spice, and are thinner and flatter than Eccles cakes. The top is brushed with milk and sprinkled with sugar before baking.

Goosnargh Cakes.

Goosnargh Cakes originated in the village of the same name and are still made and sold in the local shop. They are thick shortbread biscuits, flavoured with coriander and carraway seeds and the tops are heavily dusted with fine sugar.

Lancashire Cheese.

Lancashire cheese is a popular and rich delicacy. It can be bought either mild or "tasty", the latter being of a strong flavour. In spite of competition from continental and fancy cheeses, Lancashire cheese is still a firm favourite and can be found in all the grocery shops and markets. Cheese and pickled onions are available in country inns throughout the county, while cheese and apple pie are traditional Lancashire fare which go well together.

Lytham Shrimps.

Lytham shrimps are a great delicacy. They are boiled and then "topped and tailed" by hand in the homes of the shrimp pickers, for no machine has yet been invented which can do the job effectively.

Ormskirk Gingerbread and Potatoes.

These are sold in this ancient town which was granted a Thursday market and a five-day fair by King Edward I in 1286. Today the market is held in the main street and has over 200 stalls, and during the summer coaches bring holidaymakers from Lancashire coast resorts.

Tripe.

Tripe is another popular dish in the area. Lancashire tripe is bleached and cooked and can be eaten cold as bought. Tripe and onions is made by cooking the tripe in milk and then adding a sauce from cooked onions, cornflour and milk. This is very nourishing and cheap. Tripe on a skewer used to be sold in Bolton at the fair every January 1st, together with black peas.

Trotters.

Trotters of pigs and the feet of sheep are boiled and skinned, cooked with onions and served with a white sauce made from the stock, or eaten cold.

Wigan Hindle Wakes.

If true to its name, this savoury meal was probably served as a treat during the Wakes Week when people would have money to spend and would be on holiday. It consists of chicken stuffed with breadcrumbs and prunes, and boiled in water and vinegar with brown sugar. It is served cold with lemon sauce and could be a welcome addition to any picnic basket.

3: Legends, Ghosts and Witches

The Witch of Bernshaw Tower.

At Castle Clough there once stood Hapton Tower, the family home of Lord William who had vowed to win the heart of Lady Sybil, the proud maiden of Bernshaw Tower. The tower stood between Burnley and Todmorden near Eagle Crag, a place associated with witches and frequented by Lady Sybil who would sit day-dreaming. One day a being appeared wishing to know her desires, and when it grasped her hand she felt a burning sensation. It told her that on the night of each All-Hallows she must become a witch and join their feast. She could however hide under any disguise which would remain until midnight when her spells would become powerless and harm could befall her. The next day she was discovered on the precipice with an injured hand.

Lord William had meanwhile sought help in his quest from a witch called Mause, who told him that her spells were useless as Lady Sybil was also a witch. But on All-Hallows she could be overcome, and Lord William and Mause therefore worked out a plan.

The following All-Hallows day Lord William went hunting with his hounds through the forests of Rossendale. A white deer was seen racing towards Eagle Crag and was brought down by a strange hound which had earlier joined the pack. Lord William put a rope round the deer's neck and took it home to Hapton Tower. At midnight a terrible shriek was heard and Lady Sybil was found where the deer had been. After confessing to a holy man, she was re-baptised before marrying Lord William.

All was well until the following eve of All-Hallows in 1632 when Lady Sybil knew that she must renew her allegiance with the devil. During the day Lord William was approached by Giles Dickisson, a miller in the village of Cliviger. Once Giles had been a happy man, but his wife Goody who longed to have a child had grown churlish and bad tempered. One evening a woman called Mal Spenser, known to be of a witch had spoken to his wife and he suspected that she too had become a witch. Giles felt that he could bear the mill no longer. His servant Robin, who was not afraid, therefore took possession of the mill. Lord William asked Robin to keep watch that night, and this he agreed to do.

That evening Lady Sybil left Bernshaw Tower and met the other witches, but during the meeting her conscience rebelled. There was a rush and a scream as the crowd scattered leaving her unconscious. Meanwhile Robin was watching at the mill when a number of cats, bats and other hideous things suddenly attacked him. He fought back and a cat's paw fell to the floor. Next morning he took this to Lord William, but when he uncovered it he found instead a human hand wearing a wedding ring. The nobleman recognised the ring as his wife's and demanded to see her hand, but she refused to show him. He then raised his sword to kill her but could not and instead took her in his arms and forgave her. Then she held up her hand, which was whole once more but with a mark round the wrist and with her wedding ring missing. Thus forgiven she peacefully died. According to the legend Lady Sybil was buried by Eagle Crag, and it is said that on the eve of All-Hallows the hound and the white deer still meet there with a huntsman in full chase.

"The Dule Upo' Dun."

THREE miles from Clitheroe on the road to Waddington there stood a public house with the sign of the devil on horseback. This sign had its origins in an interesting legend. Michael Waddington, a tailor, spent most of his money at the inn, and one evening sat wishing aloud for more money so that he could have another drink. A stranger dressed in black entered, sat down at one side of the fire and stared at the tailor with bright piercing eyes. Michael changed his seat, but still the stranger stared until eventually the tailor left the inn.

On his way home Michael was followed by the stranger, who promised him all the money and drink he wanted without having to work. He told the tailor to say three aves, the creed and the paternoster backwards three times and to call on an invisible demon who would tell him what to do. This Michael did and when the devil appeared he was granted three wishes if he first signed a contract with him. If the tailor signed he could live for seven years, but if not he would die immediately, so Michael signed with a drop of blood.

When he arrived home he felt very low, and his wife in trying to cheer him up said she wished there was more food for supper. Immediately food appeared on the table. "I wish you were far away," the frightened tailor remarked and his wife disappeared. The tailor wished that his wife would come back, and when she returned he admitted he had wasted his three wishes and sold his soul to the devil. He promised that for the next seven years he would drink no more.

During this period Michael worked hard and earned a lot of money, and when the seventh year came to a close he went to a holy man who told him to repent and pray. Michael then told the devil that he had been cheated into selling his soul, so the devil agreed to grant him one more wish. Looking outside Michael saw a dun horse grazing, and he wished that the devil would ride away on it and never bother him again. Immediately the horse galloped away with the devil on its back. Michael lived to an old age, and when he died his family turned his home into a public house having *The Dule Upo' Dun* for a sign.

The Haunted Hall.

CHINGLE HALL in the village of Goosnargh, near Preston, is reputed to be haunted to this day. Mysterious footsteps have been heard both inside and outside the hall, flowers are moved, doors opened and the figure of a monk seen.

According to legend a certain John Wall was born at Chingle Hall in 1620. He was sent abroad to study for admission to the priesthood in Douai and Rome, where he was ordained in 1645. In 1661 he joined the Brothers of the Order of St. Francis before taking up missionary work in the Midlands with Father Leo Randolph. John Wall became a victim of the Titus Oates plot and, though never proved guilty, was hung, drawn and quartered at Worcester on the 22nd August, 1679. He was acclaimed a Martyr of the Catholic Church.

After his execution his head was taken to Father Randolph for preservation and then to Douai. The Poor Clare nuns brought it back to England during the French Revolution, but at this point opinion is divided. One theory is that the nuns sent the head to Chingle Hall for burial before returning to France. Another theory claims that they returned it to a convent on the Continent in 1834 and buried it in the garden. Eventually however a member of the Wall family gained possession of the head and buried it at Chingle Hall. It has never been found, but the unhappy spirit of John Wall is said to be the cause of the disturbances which still continue at the Hall. This building is situated on the B5269 road, and may be visited providing an appointment is made beforehand with the present owner, Mrs. M. Howarth. (See Events, p. 66).

The Lost Farm.

NOTHING now remains of the Lost Farm or the outbuildings, but they are believed to have stood on the coast of Lancashire somewhere in the region of Southport or Formby. According to legend the farm was inhabited by a farmer and fisherman called George Grimes, who lived with his wife, his beautiful daughter

Katherine and a dumb servant called Dick who had been at the farm for a year. This servant could hear and chalked his replies, but people thought the marks he made were evil.

One stormy night Grimes and the servant set out to go fishing. Grimes was furious when he discovered the boat was being rowed back to shore by a stranger, who gave him a gold piece and said he had borrowed the boat to get rid of something which had been plaguing him. Grimes and the servant then set off, the wind having reached gale force. When they drew in their nets they were astonished to find a heavy casket among the fish; Grimes who was very greedy thought he had found treasure and immediately set off for home. On reaching the farmhouse he put the casket in a chest by his bed, but during the storm the building was struck by lightning and Grimes uneasily remembered that the stranger had been so glad to get rid of the casket. Katherine meanwhile realised that Dick had not returned, and on hearing a whispering noise coming from the bedroom she went to investigate and discovered the casket. She took it to her father who ordered her to return it to the bedroom, but as she was replacing it in the chest she was certain that it moved and she fled from the room terrified. Then the whispering began again.Suddenly the bedroom door opened and Dick appeared; he refused to tell them where he had been and before they could pursue the matter further a flash of lightning set fire to the barn roof. More misfortunes followed, and one day Katherine and Dick disappeared.

After this Grimes decided to throw the casket into the sea, but no sooner had he returned to the shore than he saw it following him on the tide. He returned to the farm to bury it in a deep hole, but when this had been done dreadful noises came from the box and soon everyone had heard them. No-one now dared to go past the farm at night, and it became known as "Lost Farm". When Grimes left no-one else would live there. Some weeks later Grimes went to Preston searching for his daughter, and was amazed to find Katherine involved in a plot to free Dick who had been taken prisoner. He reluctantly agreed to help and Dick, who was really the Earl of Derwentwater, made his escape to the Irish Channel where a ship was waiting for him. Katherine returned home with her father, and no more was heard of the casket.

Mab's Cross at Wigan.

MAB'S CROSS still stands in front of the Woodfield Junior School in Standishgate, Wigan. The legend connected with it concerns Sir William Bradshaigh and his wife Lady Mabel of Haigh Hall near Wigan. In 1314 Sir William rode away to join the war with the Scots and nothing was heard of him for ten years Lady Mabel presuming him to be dead, married a Welsh knight, Sir Osmund Nevill.

Ten years after leaving, Sir William returned disguised as a pilgrim and went among the people enquiring about Lady Mabel. He was told that she had been forced to marry the Welsh knight and was unhappy for he was very harsh towards her. It was said that on finding her crying over a souvenir of Sir William he had cruelly burned it in front of her. Sir William was also told that the knight had threatened to turn Lady Mabel and her children from their home if she did not marry him, for Sir Osmund claimed he had been given Sir William's lands by the Earl of Lancaster for serving him faithfully. When "the pilgrim" heard that this was the birthday of the late Sir William and that Lady Mabel would be giving out alms to the poor, he went to the hall in his disguise. Lady Mabel was in deep mourning and he waited until last before bowing low and giving her his signet ring. Her Ladyship begged to be told where her husband's body was buried so that she might go there, but Sir William reminded her that she was married to another. Lady Mabel replied that she was unhappy and clung to the memory of her late husband. Then Sir William said her name, "Mabel Bradshaigh", repeated it and threw off his hood. Lady Mabel rushed towards him, but before she could reach his arms the Welsh knight appeared with his bowmen and took Sir William to the dungeons.

Suddenly the great bell of Haigh Hall was heard ringing loudly. One of Sir William's faithful servants had recognised him despite his disguise, and had rung the bell which was used in times of trouble. Immediately the local people seized their weapons and rushed to the hall where they freed Sir William. The Welsh knight had fled, but his aggressor followed and slew him in single combat at Newton. For this Sir William was outlawed from Haigh Hall for a further year and a day, but he and Lady Mabel lived happily together when they were at last re-united. Her conscience was however so stricken over her bigamous marriage to the Welsh knight that she walked in penance every week, barefooted and barelegged, to the cross in Standishgate. Her troubled spirit is said to still walk this path and haunt a gallery at the hall. The tomb of Sir William and Lady Mabel Bradshaigh is to be seen in Wigan Parish Church. (See Wigan Parish Church, p. 43; Haigh Hall, p. 35.)

Meg the Witch.

MEG SHELTON was born at Singleton, a village in the Fylde, and lived most of her life at Cuckoo Hall Cottage in nearby Wesham. She was a traditional witch who terrorised the local farmers by spoiling their crops and turning the milk sour. According to legend she was seen stealing corn, and at the sight of the approaching farmer turned herself into a stook. The farmer, noticing the extra stook, was so furious that he drove a pitchfork into the corn and Meg rode away on a broomstick holding a bleeding arm.

When she died she was taken to St. Anne's Church, Woodplumpton, to be buried. Three times she scratched her way to the surface, until eventually the ground was exorcised and she was re-buried face downwards. A large stone was then placed on top of her grave to prevent any further escapes. The grave is still to be seen at the church and it is said that anyone dancing round it will have a wish granted. (See Woodplumpton Church, p. 44).

Pendle Hill.

THE most famous stories of Lancashire concern the witches of Pendle Hill, the brooding and dark mass which brings readily to mind the names of Old Chattox, Old Demdike and the Device family. To avert the witches' spells the God-fearing folk of Pendle collected charms such as horse shoes which were hung over stable doors to protect the animals, and doors and windows were built with crooked frames to prevent the devil from passing through them. In the village of Worston is a cottage with a circular window, known as a witchs' window, set high in the wall. Stones with holes in them were treasured and hung as amulets for good luck, and when the cows were turned loose into the fields each spring the farmers would plait their tails with red thread to stop the witches milking them. Dough was marked with the sign of the cross to protect it from the witches' charms, and a red-hot iron would be dipped into the churn to expel any witch who might have hidden there before the cream was made. The west wall of the church at Newchurch-in-Pendle contains an oval window resembling a human eye, which is said to have been placed there to avert the "evil eye" of the Pendle witches. A shop in the village of Newchurch sells models of witches astride broomsticks.

How much is superstition and how much fact? No-one knows. But Pendle Hill still retains an atmosphere of evil, and at times the words "emen hetan" which were supposed to give the witches their magic powers can almost be heard. Only the bravest dare walk up the slopes of Pendle, as is tradition, on the night of Hallowe'en. Pendle Hill is situated due east of the A59 at Clitheroe.

The White Lady of Samlesbury Hall.

SAMLESBURY HALL, near Preston, is still said to be haunted by the ghost of Lady Dorothy Southworth. She was the daughter of Sir John Southworth, a strict Roman Catholic, and fell in love with the son of an equally strict Protestant. The couple were forbidden to marry and planned to elope, but their plans were overheard by one of Lady Dorothy's brothers. At the time set for their escape the Southworth family surprised the couple, and killed the young knight whose body was secretly buried. Lady Dorothy was sent abroad to a convent, where she died of a broken heart. Some years ago a human skeleton was discovered in the grounds of Samlesbury Hall, which is thought to have been that of the unfortunate young knight. Lady Dorothy's ghost, a woman in white, has been seen on occasions inside the hall and in the grounds outside. (See Samlesbury Hall, p. 32).

Smithills Hall, Bolton.

SMITHILLS HALL is the setting for two rather gruesome stories, both concerning footprints. According to legend, the first footprint was made by a former owner of Smithills Hall who was determined by any means to prolong his life. After many calculations he decided that for him to live indefinitely a life should be sacrificed every thirty years. He planned to kill a young female relative who had been orphaned and placed in his care and protection. He took her to a wood near the hall where he stabbed her and buried her body, but in carrying out this evil deed the old man trod in the girl's blood. As he walked home his footsteps were marked by a bloody imprint which showed inside the hall, thus arousing such suspicion in the minds of his servants that the old man fled. When at last he returned, his first footsteps inside the hall were traced in blood—a horrifying reminder of his crime. Although he died a long time ago, the bloody footprints are still said to re-appear from time to time to trace the old man's guilty steps through the house.

The second legend concerns George Marsh who in 1554 was accused of heresy. As his mother and brother had been threatened, he went voluntarily to Smithills to stand trial before the magistrate Sir Roger Barton and a priest. He was tried in an upper room at the hall, known as the Green Room, and was found guilty. As he was being taken downstairs he met a number of his relations who begged him to renounce his beliefs, but Marsh refused and stamped his foot on the floor to declare his faith. He was then brought before Lord Derby, again found guilty and taken to Lancaster. From here he was moved to Chester, and after a further trial was burnt at the stake just outside the city boundary in April 1555. The footprint he made at Smithills Hall appears as a cavity in a flag stone and can still be seen. This flag was reputedly once removed as a prank, but during the night hideous noises were heard which did not cease until the stone was replaced. It is thought that Marsh may have preached in the church at Deane, just outside Bolton, and a carving near the altar shows him dying at the stake at Chester. (See Smithills Hall, p. 23).

The Ghost of Waddow Hall.

THE grounds of Waddow Hall, near Waddington, are the scene of a mysterious legend concerning a servant girl at the hall called

Peg O'Nell. Near the bank of the river Ribble is a spring named Peg O'Nell's well, and by it stands a headless stone figure supposed to be a monument to her. According to the legend, Idle Peg one day went to fetch some water, after quarrelling with her mistress, who told her that she hoped she would fall and break her neck. Outside it was very frosty, and by the well Peg did indeed fall and was killed. Her spirit thereafter haunted the house, and every seven years any traveller crossing the river would mysteriously die. On Peg's night a bird, dog or cat would be drowned in the river as a sacrifice to her tormented soul.

Peg's mistress in the meantime had a son presumed to be possessed of demons, so she sent for a priest to exorcise this spirit and grew anxious when he failed to arrive. The preacher was eventually found half-drowned in the river, and at this the mistress went out and knocked the head off the monument to Peg. Although this seemed to quell Peg's turbulent spirit, a cock was nevertheless sacrificed each year in Peg's room.

In the West Riding of Yorkshire on the B6478, 1½ miles north of Clitheroe, Waddow Hall is now used as a training centre for adult members of the Girl Guides.

4: Places of Interest

Blackpool Zoological Gardens.

Opening: Spring 1972 at East Park Drive; admission: proposed 40p.

SCHEDULED to open to the public in the spring of 1972, the zoo will initially cover 17 acres and will later be enlarged to 32 acres. Amenities will include catering facilities and picnic areas, together with ample car parking. Among the attractions will be a children's zoo containing an exotic animal house and a "Kinder Kasba" village for small animal handling; a small exhibit hall for miscellaneous children's pets; a pool for waterfowl, together with a Noah's Ark feature; and a riding ring with donkey and pony stables and enclosures. Many other animals and birds will be on show in natural surroundings, including Cuban flamingoes, waterfowl of all kinds, Bactrian camels, Axis deer, North American wapiti and white tailed deer, Prairie marmots and Barbary wild sheep. In a large pool there will be Californian sea-lions. There will be a small section of the proposed primate house containing spider monkeys, gibbons, squirrel monkeys and many others. A macaw and toucan aviary will in addition house hyacinthine and palm cockatoos.

This information has been kindly supplied by the Blackpool County Borough Council and may be liable to variation before the opening of the Zoo.

Blackstone Edge Roman Road.

South of the A58 Littleborough to Ripponden (Yorkshire) road.

GENERALLY supposed to be of Roman origin, this road passes over the moors and the Yorkshire border reaching to a height of 1,475 feet at its peak. It is made of rough paving approximately 15ft wide and has central troughed stones. From its rather sudden start on the Lancashire side the road can be traced in a straight line, much being visible and in a good state of repair. The reason for the central trough is obscure and various arguments have been put forward, the main one being that it was filled with soil to stop horses from sliding on the steep gradient.

Bleasdale Circle.
Route: From Lancaster on A6. Turn at Garstang for Oakenclough; signpost for Bleasdale.

AT the beginning of this century a moorland burial spot dating from the early Bronze Age was uncovered at Bleasdale. Here enormous wooden posts were found which formed a prehistoric burial circle over 3,000 years ago. To prevent the wood from deteriorating the blocks were removed to the Harris Museum at Preston where some of the timbers may be seen, and concrete posts of a similar size were erected in their place. Further excavations revealed the remains of two more circles, an outer ring approximately 150 feet in diameter of oak logs and a smaller ring of birch poles. These were laid flat in the bottom of the ditch surrounding the inner ring of oak posts. It was in the smaller ring that the eleven massive oak posts were discovered near the point where the two outer circles met. This innermost circle had an entrance flanked by two even larger oak posts making it into the shape of a horseshoe. Within this innermost circle of horseshoe form, two funeral or cinerary urns containing human ashes and bones were uncovered. These urns were also removed to the Harris Museum. Bleasdale Circle is an example of a "palisaded barrow" and the innermost circle of posts probably represents a "house of the dead". Parallels for these palisaded barrows can be found in Holland and North Germany. The fact that the original wooden posts still exist make it unique. The ring of concrete posts marking the burial circle stand in a lonely and desolate spot in the heart of the Bleasdale fells; the setting is most impressive and it is easy to imagine primitive man worshipping here.

Hall-i'-th'-Wood, Bolton.
The Bolton ring-road, A58, passes the door. Open April to September, 10 a.m.–6 p.m., Sundays 2 p.m.–6 p.m., closed Thursdays; October to March, 10 a.m.–5 p.m., closed Thursdays and Sundays. Car park and cafe during summer.

AS one approaches this old Tudor manor house, the inaptitude of its name seems amusing. However, since the date of its erection in the latter half of the 15th century until up to a hundred years ago it was surrounded by a thick belt of trees. Now it stands like a small island amid a sea of modern houses and arterial roads, Despite this, when standing in the small courtyard one can almost feel the sense of peace and the air of quiet security which often emanates from such old buildings.

The different periods and architectural styles through which Hall-i'-th'-Wood has lived are clearly shown. The original half-timbered post and plaster portion was built by the first Lawrence

Hall-i'-th'-Wood, Bolton.

Brownlow and now forms the East Wing. Additions were next made during the Elizabethan period; at the time of the Civil Wa.ı the west side was demolished and a new south-west wing rebuilt.

Eventually the hall passed by marriage to the Starkey family, who lived here until the 18th century. It was at this time that the character of the building changed. In 1779, when Samuel Crompton produced the prototype of his spinning mule which was to revolutionise the cotton industry and bring prosperity to Lancashire, it was occupied by poor tenant farmers.

Viscount Leverhulme bought Hall-i'-th'-Wood in 1900 and, after restoration, presented it to Bolton Corporation thus making it available to the public as a folk museum. The various rooms have been carefully furnished with period pieces acquired from all over Lancashire and further afield. Since the architectural additions made by the past owners fall into definite historical periods, the furnishing of the rooms in each wing of the hall gives a comprehensive view of life throughout the centuries. One room is solely devoted to Samuel Crompton and contains many of his personal possessions; his clock, the chamber organ which he made, books containing several of the hymns composed while he was choirmaster of the Swedenborgain Chapel, and a small scale model of his spinning mule. Perhaps one of the most poignant reminders of his invention is in part of the hall not open to visitors—a small space beneath the rafters. It was here that Crompton hid his machine on the night when mill workers hammered at the doors with fists and sticks, frightened by the thought that mechanisation would rob them of their livelihood. The many other exhibits are too numerous to mention in detail, but range from furniture and fire irons to kitchen utensils and musical instruments and are all wonderfully preserved.

Smithills Hall, Bolton.

Route: Bolton ring-road, A58. Opening times April to September, weekdays, 10 a.m.–6 p.m., closed on Thursdays; October to March, weekdays, 10 a.m.–5 p.m., closed on Thursdays and Sundays. Admission free.

SMITHILLS HALL is one of the oldest manor houses in Lancashire, the first documented ownership being by the Knights Hospitallers from whom it was held by Richard de Hulton. The next owner was William de Radclyffe and this family name is associated with the hall until 1485 when it passed by marriage to John Barton and his heirs. In 1723 it was sold to Joseph Byrom and 78 years later passed to the Ainsworth family who held the property for the next 130 years. Finally Bolton Corporation bought Smithills Hall in 1938.

The Great Hall with the small wing adjoining to the east is all that remains of the 14th century timber-framed structure. Its interior shows the open timber roof with "quatrefoil" decoration, and the "spares" or projecting walls carrying the roof arch. Originally there must have been a roof aperture for smoke to escape from a centrally placed open fire, but now the only indication is a stout metal log support around which blazing timbers were once heaped. In the 16th century Andrew Barton considerably enlarged the house, building the east wing with its withdrawing room and bedrooms above. The panelling in the withdrawing room contains some fine examples of linenfold carving, one panel showing a "rebus" or pictorial pun on the name of Barton. This room also contains a moulded oak beam ceiling, an oriel window and a set of the coats of arms of various owners of Smithills—these were painted in the 19th century during the Ainsworth's occupation. Services are still held in the chapel which was destroyed by fire and rebuilt in 1856 to the old plan. There is an interesting east window with heraldic glass including the Royal Arms of a Tudor sovereign, possibly Elizabeth I, and also those of Thomas Cranmer when Archbishop of Canterbury. At the entrance to the chapel passage is a clearly defined footprint said to be that of George Marsh, accused of heresy in 1555 (see Ghosts and Witches, p. 18).

There are car park facilities and also a restaurant in the grounds, a few yards from the hall.

The Trough of Bowland

IT comes as a pleasant surprise to visitors to Lancashire to find a wild upland region on the edge of the Forest of Bowland known to its frequent visitors as "The Trough." Running through the valley is the river Hodder which eventually joins the Ribble, and the scenery is varied from wild moorland to parkland, forest, gentle valleys with mountain streams and quiet open spaces with views of craggy hills.

Approaching the region from the south, the Longridge Road takes one to the pleasant village of Chipping. Here the old school-house dated 1684 and the ancient and interesting church of St. Bartholomew can be seen. The church was rebuilt in 1506 and restored in 1872. In the grounds are a Saxon holy water stoup and a sun dial dated 1708. Parlick Pike probably one of the best summits in Bowland, stands over Chipping. Uninterrupted views of the Vale of Chipping, Bleasdale and the Fylde plain can be seen.

The Chipping to Whitewell road winds in and out of the boundary between Lancashire and Yorkshire, and Browsholme Hall, although on Yorkshire soil has a Lancashire address (see page 27). The hamlet of Whitewell, situated on the river Hodder, is renowned for its magnificent scenery. At St. Michael's Church there is a notice telling visitors that part of the parish is in Lancashire and part in Yorkshire. The river Hodder and its tributaries, the Dunsop and the Langden Beck, meet at Dunsop Bridge which is a pleasant picnicing spot. Nearby is a trout farm where trout in all stages of growth are kept in tanks and used to restock rivers and sold to angling clubs. Leedham's Garage at Dunsop Bridge run a bus service from Clitheroe to Slaidburn via Bashall Eaves, Cow Ark, Whitewell, Dunsop Bridge, Newton and Slaidburn. There is no Sunday service but parties of 20 will be taken if arrangements are made with the garage.

The Trough of Bowland shows the north country at its best and at the county border the road passes between the peaks of Whins Brow (1,565 feet) and Fell Top (1,568 feet). At the highest point is a small observation tower. Continuing towards Lancaster just off the main road, is the Shepherd's Church of Abbeystead with its beautiful stained glass windows depicting shepherds and their flocks. Pegs can still be seen in the porch where shepherds hung their crooks. Next to the church stands a public stable built by Thomas Townley in the 17th century. Between Abbeystead and Lancaster there is a small observation tower with panoramic views. The scenery changes from deep valleys to wild moorland, seen at its greatest beauty in the Autumn.

Carved reredos in the Townley Chapel, Townley Hall, Burnley.

Townley Hall, Burnley.
On A6114 due south of Burnley. Opens 10 a.m.–5.30 p.m., summer; 10 a.m.–5 p.m., winter; 2 p.m.–5 p.m., Sundays all the year. Admission: Guided tours by appointment—not available on Sundays or Bank Holidays. Refreshments and car parking.

TOWNLEY HALL, originally built as a hunting lodge for the Deans of Whalley, dates back mainly to the 16th century, although the south side was probably built in the 14th century.

Loyalty to the throne and the Church brought much sorrow to the Townley family, who were once both wealthy and powerful. John Townley, old and blind and deprived of large sums of money, was imprisoned in many parts of the country. He was finally forced to remain within five miles of Townley. In 1601 he completed the doorway to the beautiful private chapel, and his work can be seen to this day. In the wall of the chapel lined entirely with oak, is a grilled panel; it was from here Lady Frances Townley saw her husband's head displayed, after it had hung on Temple Bar. In the ante-room are five beautifully embroidered medieval vestments from Whalley Abbey.

The house has many other interesting features. The entrance hall has a beautiful 18th century ceiling and walls decorated with shields of Roman Emperors. In the thickness of the walls is a priest's hiding-place with stairs leading to the gallery above where armour from many countries is set against magnificent panelling. The Hall, now an Art Gallery and Museum is completely furnished and contains many valuable art treasures including the lovely chairs which belonged to Lord Byron. In the kitchens are to be seen utensils used up to 300 years ago. Among the many art treasures are paintings by Turner, Landseer and Fielding, and a study by Croft of Oliver Cromwell after the battle at Marston Moor. There is also a natural history collection of birds and animals.

Astley Hall, Chorley.

On A6, eight miles south of Preston; entrance opposite Parish Church. Open weekdays and Sundays, May to August, 2 p.m.–8 p.m.; April and September, 2 p.m.–6 p.m.; weekdays only, October to March, 2 p.m.–4 p.m. Admission, 2½p. (free on Tuesdays and Thursdays).

THE 16th-century Astley Hall is situated in a beautiful park with lake and woodlands, and is built round a central courtyard to which additions and improvements have been made over the years. The Great Hall rises for two storeys and, with the drawing room, has magnificent and lavishly ornamental plaster ceilings of the 17th century. Both rooms contain many fine paintings and portraits. In 1666 the famous Flemish tapestries depicting the "Quest of the Golden Fleece" were brought to the hall, and these now hang in the drawing room.

The New Gallery has a permanent collection of pictures, pottery and glass, and during the summer months loan exhibitions are held. The Long Gallery contains a remarkable shovel-board table, 23½ft. long with twenty legs, and unsurpassed for its elaborate embellishment. Among many other priceless treasures is the "Cromwell Bed", the best preserved oak four-poster bed in the country. (See also Chorley Church, p. 36.)

Clitheroe Castle.

The grounds and remains of the castle are open to the public. Admittance is free.

CLITHEROE CASTLE, built by the Normans on a limestone knoll overlooking the town, is one of the oldest stone structures within the county and has the smallest Norman keep in England. The site was chosen after the Conquest by Roger de Poitou, the first Lord of the Honor of Clitheroe, and from here he administered the land given to him by the Conqueror. Several courts were held here, although important matters were always referred to Lancaster. The castle was also used as a prison and a place of worship, having both a jailor and a priest.

In 1644 the fortress was taken by the Royalists, and from here they raided the surrounding countryside. After Cromwell defeated the Royalist army at Preston, an order was sent out that the castle at Clitheroe was to be destroyed, thus removing any future threat, and consequently the gatehouse and chapel were demolished. In 1920 the remains were bought by the town, the grounds now being a war memorial. The keep is open to the public and it is possible to walk on top of the surrounding curtain wall.

There is a legend attached to Clitheroe Castle concerning a large hole which can still be seen in the wall of the keep. This is said to have been caused by the devil who one day strode from Hambledon Hill to Deerstones Quarry near Sabden. This quarry contains an outcrop of sandstone rock, and on a large boulder are two marks which are supposedly footprints made by the Devil. From here he walked to a hill crest nearer Clitheroe, on top of which is a large heap of stones. From this hill the Devil hoped to throw stones at the Castle. He stood with an apronful of stones, and with one of them hit the Castle wall. As he threw the stone the strings of his apron broke and the stones fell in a heap on the ground. The hill still bears the name—the Devil's Apronful.

Browsholme Hall, near Clitheroe.

Continue north off B6246 from Whalley. Open Thursdays, Saturdays and Sundays all the year; Tuesdays from Good Friday to mid-October and all Bank Holiday Mondays. Admission 17½p; no reduction for children. Car park free; restaurant facilities in the area.

THE home of the Parker family is a beautiful example of an English country mansion dating from early Tudor times, and is a long three-storied building with the rooms wainscotted with oak. Features of the hall are the magnificent Elizabethan and Stuart panelling and a window made of fragments from Whalley Abbey. There is a superb collection of paintings, silver and old china, tapestries and many other objects of historical interest. Suits of armour dating back to the Battle of Hastings are on display in the central hall. Of special interest is a gauge used to measure the feet of every dog before it was allowed into the Forest of Bowland; if the poor animal's feet proved too large it was mutilated to prevent it hunting the deer. Thomas Lister Parker spent over £100,000 landscaping the magnificent gardens early in the 19th century. Tours are now conducted by the present owner, Colonel Robert Parker. (See also Whalley Abbey, p. 33, and Whalley church, p. 42.)

Martholme Gatehouse, Great Harwood, Blackburn.
Exterior open Mondays, Fridays and Saturdays. Interoir open by appointment only, phone Great Harwood 2809. Admission, 15p.

THE gatehouse was erected in 1561 as the entrance to a large manor house which had been built in the 14th century. Records show that extensive repairs were made at the same time to the existing Great Hall which was owned by Thomas Hesketh. It seems likely that he was also responsible for the insertion of windows in the gables of the house facing the gatehouse, since they display the same style of workmanship. Some 50 years later a new east wing was added and an additional outer gateway was built. Martholme remained the property of the Hesketh family until the 17th century when it was being used as a dower house, the main residence of the family then being Rufford Old Hall. After this period very little is known of the history of the gatehouse, except that it appears to have been used as a tenant farmhouse until the Hesketh sold the property to the Trappes-Lomax family who owned it until 1925. The 16th century structure fell into disrepair, and it was virtually a ruin until its restoration in 1969.

Hoghton Tower.
On the A675 Preston–Blackburn road. Open; Thursday, Saturday and Sunday from June to September, 2 p.m.–5 p.m. Admissions adults 5p, children 2½p.

HOGHTON TOWER was built on high ground round two courtyards in about 1563, and from its grey walls the Welsh mountains and the Yorkshire moors can be seen on a clear day. The Hoghton family history is mainly one of revelry and hunting. In 1617 King James I enjoyed a day's hunting to such an extent that he gave the Holcombe Hunt the honour of wearing his own scarlet livery, and the right to hunt "for ever" on a specified number of days in the forest. It was here also that he knighted a loin of beef "Sir Loin".

The men of Lancashire presented a petition to King James I at Hoghton Tower requesting the restoration of archery, leaping and

Entrance gate to Hoghton Tower.

Morris dancing on Sundays. These had been forbidden by the Puritans; the king accepted the petition and restored everything except bear baiting, bull baiting and bowls. The Civil War brought sorrow to the Hoghton family, and in the reign of Elizabeth I Thomas Hoghton went into exile for his beliefs. The house was abandoned in the 18th century, later restored, and is still occupied by a member of the de Hoghton family.

Ribchester, Roman Fort, Museum and Church.
On B6245 south of Longridge. Museum open daily, 2 p.m.–6 p.m. Admission: 7½p.

AS its present day name suggests, Ribchester was a Roman fortified encampment on the banks of the river Ribble. Built by Agricola about 80 AD and known as Bremetennacum, it was a defence outpost against the Brigantes, the then inhabitants of Lancashire and Yorkshire and against marauders from Ireland whose shallow sea-going boats could encroach along the Ribble. When first built the fort covered about five and three-quarter acres surrounded by clay ramparts which had a base width of fifteen feet and tapered toward the summit. These were surmounted by palisading, watch towers and Balistae platforms, recent work in the Rectory gardens having uncovered one of the Balista Stones which is a missile of four pounds weight.

About 1,000 men—cohorts from the different legions occupying Britain—were stationed at Bremetennacum. The northern forts were linked by straight and well metalled roads, and portions of these can clearly be seen today running from Ribchester towards Chester, Manchester, Lancaster and York. Bremetennacum underwent many structural changes during the period of the Roman occupation; stone walls replaced clay ramparts and the further protection of a Fosse or moat was added, the remains of which are still visible at the west end of the churchyard.

The Ribchester of today lives gently in the memory of its past. The museum, built in 1914, now houses most of the antiquities which have been discovered throughout the years, the exception being a spectacular bronze helmet found in a remarkable state of preservation. Only a replica is on display, the original being in the British Museum. There is, however, a wonderful collection of objects which bring to life the human side of history—pottery, rings, a game of discs played by the soldiers and even an altar to "the holy God Apollo Maponus" asking for safety of the "horsemen of Bremetennacum". At the main entrance to the museum are several pillars which had formed part of the Roman baths situated behind what is now the *White Bull Inn.* When the baths were excavated the usual hypocaust and steps were found; the perforated terracotta warming tiles were still intact and these were later placed in the museum.

The Ribchester helmet at Ribchester Museum.

Ribchester's parish church and churchyard are built out of and on top of the larger stone remains of Roman times, but even the first tiny chapel probably did not come into existence until about 100 years after the withdrawal of the legions. There is however one slender trace which could possibly link some Roman soldier and his family with the newly-emerging Christian faith—a Roman lamp bearing the Chrisma monogram. For those interested in archaeology, "digs" are still in progress at Ribchester and all enquiries should be made at the museum.

Rufford Old Hall.

Rufford Old Hall.
On east side of A59, five miles north of Ormskirk. Open all year, weekdays (except Mondays), 12 noon–8 p.m. or dusk. Sundays, 1 p.m.–8 p.m. or dusk. Closed Wednesdays, October 1st to March 31st, and Thursdays between December 1st and January 31st. Admission, adults 15p, children 10p if accompanied by an adult. Car park and cafe.

RECENTLY given to the National Trust, this beautiful black and white half-timbered medieval manor house is well worth a visit. It has remained practically unaltered since it was built in 1480, and has a magnificent hammerbeamed roof. The interior of the hall contains many examples of rich carving, the most notable being the timbered screen with its ornate Gothic carving. There are collections of 17th century furniture, 16th century arms and armour, old English coins and beautiful tapestries from Brussels and Mortlake. Among all this wealth of history, the Ashcroft Museum—also in part of the hall—shows the domestic and industrial life of Lancashire in former times. Displays of period costumes and Victoriana are also to be found here.

Samlesbury Hall.
On A59 Preston–Blackburn road. Open: Sundays from 2 p.m. Admission: Adults 10p, children 5p. Parking, afternoon tea available.

BUILT in 1325 by Gilbert Southworth for his bride, Samlesbury Hall remained in the family until 1679 and became one of the great houses of Lancashire as well as a stronghold of the Catholic faith. Constructed of local materials in a random mixture of timber, stone and brick, it blends well with the surroundings. A chapel was added to the Great Hall in about 1420, and in the middle of the 16th century the south-west wing was completed and many renovations took place. Above the bay or oriel window at the south-east end of the Great Hall was built a small square chamber about ten feet square, known as the "Oratory" or priest's room. It has two windows and on one side meets the slope of the roof of the great hall to form a "bolt hole". A story says that a priest was dragged from here, fought a duel and was killed. Stains on the floor were supposed to be his blood, and in the 1890s the floor had to be removed as servants would not stay in a house with such a gruesome story.

The present entrance hall has an elaborate ceiling of black oak and a Tudor fireplace. Here the entrance to another "bolt hole" has recently been found, and a ventilation brick can clearly be seen on the outside of the chimney. Also in this wing is the dining-room with a richly carved cornice and a timbered ceiling divided into sections by moulded beams. The chapel contains a large window, probably taken from Whalley Abbey at the time of the dissolution of the monastery, and there is also a very old sandstone font set on a millstone. In 1925 the hall and grounds were purchased by a Board of Trustees to be preserved for public use. The hall has been refurnished in period style and, as well as being a building of great historical interest, it is used for meetings of local societies, drama and musical performances. (See The White Lady of Samlesbury Hall, p. 17.)

Stoneyhurst College.
Take the A59 to Whalley and turn left onto B6246. Join B6243 and continue for two miles; the college is on the right. Open: The church at all times between dawn and dusk. Conducted tours of the college 2 p.m.–4.45 p.m. at weekends during the summer. Admission: 12½p. Refreshments are available nearby.

BUILT in the 16th century and set in beautiful and extensive grounds near the river Hodder, this mansion was originally the home of the Shireburne family whose coat of arms is to be seen over the main doorway. It was allowed to fall into ruins before passing to Roman Catholic refugees from France, who carefully restored it over many years and furnished it with many of their treasures. Stoneyhurst is now a famous Roman Catholic public school.

In the school museum is the cope taken by Henry VIII to the Field of the Cloth of Gold. The richly embroidered cap worn by Sir Thomas Moore is also to be seen, together with many other old and beautiful vestments. The famous library of over 30,000 volumes contains the oldest bound book in England, a 7th century copy of the Gospel according to St. John which was carried by St. Cuthbert throughout his life and buried with him in 686AD. Here also is the Book of Hours, said to have been carried by Mary, Queen of Scots to the scaffold, and a copy of Caxton's Golden Legend. The fine natural history collection was presented by Charles Waterton, the South American explorer; there is also a very well equipped observatory. The oldest possession of the school is a pagan altar found near Ribchester. (See Great Mitton Church, p. 38.)

Whalley Abbey.
On the A59 Preston to Clitheroe road. The grounds are always open to the public.

BY consent of Pope Nicholas IV, the Cistercian Order at Stanlaw, Cheshire, was granted permission in 1289 to build an abbey at Whalley. But their way was barred by the rector, of Whalley an obstinate cleric who lived until 1295. By this time Papal permission had been rescinded and a new application had to be made. The monks were anxious to move to their new slte at Whalley, and In 1297 Abbot Gregory and a party of twenty-four monks took possession of the Manor House. They intended to commence building the new abbey but again ran into opposition, this time from brother monks at nearby Sawley. It was primarily a domestic quarrel connected with local food suppliers. Sawley Abbey would need to pay more for smaller quantities now that there was a new House in the same area.

Papal procrastination, shortage of money and the unfriendly welcome of the barren countryside all hampered the construction

Gate House at Whalley Abbey.

work, and it was not until 1319 that a serious attempt at building began. First to be erected were the western gateway, chapel and guest house, all built of stone from a local quarry. The great work of building the church began in 1330, the bell tower and peal of five bells being dated 1356, but it was not until 1380 that the ceremonial first mass was celebrated within its completed walls. Construction continued slowly over the years and included the erection of a cloister court, dormitory, refectory, a bakehouse and a brewery—in fact all the various devotional and utilitarian necessities required by this self-contained community of dedicated men. If one takes the year 1444 as marking the completion of this vast project, then a total of 127 years were occupied in building the abbey.

The period from 1444 could be termed the first days of Whalley, but regrettably its "last days" were already near at hand. John Paslew was elected abbot in 1507 and he was the last to hold that office, for in 1537 he was arrested after having taken part in the Pilgrimage of Grace. He was tried for treason and executed, and in the same year the officers of Henry VIII took possession of the abbey. Today the greater part of the building is in ruins, only those portions which were rebuilt about 1603 as the Assheton Manor House remaining intact. Excavations have revealed the foundations of many of the old buildings, and from these it has been possible to gauge something of the splendour of the great monastery at the height of its glory.

The abbey grounds are now lined out with markers, but here and there the jagged bones of a wall, arch or broken fragment of pillar stand cleared of weeds as a reminder of the labour of generations of the monks of Whalley. (Also visit Whalley church, see page 42.)

Haigh Hall, Wigan.

Open daily Easter to October. Restaurant and car parking. Tractor-trailer transport from Wigan Lane.

THE owners of Haigh Hall can be traced back to 1188; in 1294 it was owned by Mabel, wife of Sir William Bradshaigh. In the early 16th century the family made considerable additions to the house, including an Elizabethan facade and an elaborately carved door attributed to Inigo Jones. At this time a substance called cannel had been found in the grounds; it burnt well and was a valuable gas producing fuel, it was also clean to touch and resembling black polished marble. The industry grew and in the 19th century further methods of transport were being sought, the project of the Leeds–Liverpool canal proving a great advance as it ran through the grounds. Some 33 boats were then owned and used, output lasted until 1860.

During the 1830s work on the hall as it is today was begun, some of the doors being made of "fumed" oak from the estate. The marble fireplaces and plaster ceilings were brought from Paris. In 1947 the hall and grounds, extending to some 244 acres, were purchased by Wigan Corporation. The plantation contains many fine horticultural features and is famous for its many rhododendrons. The main drive from Wigan Lane wanders for two miles through a fine expanse of natural woodland. There is a lily pond and a walled old English garden. (See Ghosts and Witches—Mab's Cross, p. 15, also Wigan Church, p. 43.)

5: Churches

Bradshaw: Church of St. Maxentius.
On A676 north of Bolton.

THE dedication of this church is unusual, and indeed is probably unique in the history of the Anglican Church. St. Maxentius, a 5th century abbot, was an obscure saint from a small village now named after him—St. Maixent, 34 miles from Poitiers. The reason for the dedication is obscure and open to much speculation, but can perhaps be traced back to Norman times.

Roger de Poitou, cousin of William I, was in 1094 asked to administer Lancaster in a manner previously carried out in Normandy (the town of Poitou belonged to the English crown from 1154 to 1372). By 1253 one Ughtred de Bradshaw lived in "The Hall"; he owned considerable lands in the area including "chappell fields", and thus presumably had a chapel. It seems probable that he was of Norman descent, a follower of Roger or William and had been given lands for services rendered to the crown. As the village had been named after the family, it seems natural that in the early days of their settlement they would dedicate the church to the saint of their old home town. This would strengthen the idea that the first church was built on the site early in the 12th century.

The present structure is only 98 years old, although the records go back to 1541. In the churchyard stands a tower from an earlier church of about 1500, although one of the bells is probably a century older. An old font filled with flowers is also to be seen.

Chorley: Church of St. Laurence.
On A6 between Preston and Bolton.

THE tower, chancel and nave of this church date from the mid-14th century, although the rest of the building is 19th century. A small low recess in the chancel wall was said to have contained the bones of St. Laurence, brought from Normandy by Sir Rowland Standish in 1442. The church has two fine Jacobean pews, one of which belonged to the Standish family whose funeral helmets are also to be seen. One of the two fonts is thought to be Saxon in origin, while the other is certainly medieval.

Clitheroe: Church of St. Mary Magdalene.
On A59 north of Whalley.

SET upon a hill above the town, as is the castle, a church is known to have been on this site, probably built by Roger de Poitou, in 1122, although nothing of it now remains. In the early 15th century the Norman church was pulled down and completely rebuilt. All that remains of this re-building is the tower with a fine original window above the West door, and the stone work at the east end, the 15th century church in turn being pulled down and rebuilt in 1829.

In the south aisle by the porch door is a 17th century church-warden's pew with a poor-box which was roughly carved from solid oak in 1678. On the wall is a memorial brass of 1682 to Dr. John Webster, headmaster of the local grammar school and an astrologer who wrote a book entitled *Displaying of the supposed Witchcraft*, published in 1677. The Alley Chapel contains the damaged effiges supposed to be of Sir Thomas Radcliffe and his wife. Sir Thomas was a knight who served with Henry V at Agincourt and died in 1441. The altar of the chapel is the chest-tomb of a John Morrison who died in 1718; it has a skull and crossbones engraved on the south end. The chapel window has some fragments of medieval stained glass, and the lovely 15th century east window contains stained glass showing in armorial bearings a history of the church, town and borough. On the south wall of the sanctuary can be seen the king's arms, set up in 1660. The font dates back to the 17th century, although the base is earlier. (See Clitheroe Castle, p. 26).

Eccleston Parish Church.
On B5250 off A581, approximately three miles south of Leyland.

THE parish church at Eccleston, near Chorley, is situated on the banks of the river Yarrow and is set in a neat and picturesque garden. Built about 1510, the brown stone church houses an interesting brass probably depicting the parish priest. He has a shaved crown and wears a surplice and a cope with patterned edge fastened with a large brooch. The brass, probably late 15th century, is on an altar front and is simple and pleasing. Also of note is a tie beam among the old roof timbers dating from 1334.

Great Mitton: All Hallows Church.
On B6246 north of Whalley.

THE church at Great Mitton is one of the most interesting in the Ribble valley and although situated just inside Yorkshire, it nevertheless has very strong ties with Lancashire and especially with Stoneyhurst College through the Shireburne family. The earliest part of the church is the nave dating back to 1270, the tower being added in the 15th century. In 1594 the Shireburne Chapel was built to the designs of the architect at Stoneyhurst. The Shireburne family favoured elaborate tombs and these, decorated with beautiful examples of sculpture, are situated within the chapel. A number of the inscriptions were added by the Dowager Duchess of Norfolk who was the daughter of Sir Nicholas, the last member of the family. The memorial to her father states that he was a man of great humanity and sympathy and, among other things, appointed a man to comb wool and a woman to teach the local inhabitants to spin. He allocated several rooms at Stoneyhurst for this purpose, local people being allowed to come and spin for as long as they wished. Sir Nicholas's only son, who was poisoned in the garden, has a memorial depicting two small boys, the one on the left smiling and the one on the right weeping.

The church also contains a carved oak chancel screen which may have come from Cockersand Abbey. A low side window is known as "the lepers' window", and is seemingly dedicated to the patients of a leper hospital which once stood near the Edisford Bridge. There is however some doubt about this as the hospital was closed a long time before the date of the window. There is a spacious chancel which was tiled in 1845, and the altar platform is thought to date from the same time. There are a number of old books which were at one time chained to the chapel screen. The font is not earlier than the 14th century, and bears some resemblance to a holy water stoup recently discovered in the churchyard and now placed within the Shireburne Chapel.

Hoole: Church of St. Michaels.
On A59 Preston to Southport road.

THIS small church stands on the site of a 15th century chapel of ease to St. Michaels, Croston, about three miles away. In 1642 the Royal Seal was attached to the Act rendering St. Michaels, Hoole an independent parish. The main church was built about 1628, and the south porch dates from this time; the tower was added in 1722. The church still retains its old box pews and west and south galleries; there is also an interesting two-decked pulpit with a fine sounding board dated 1695. The enormous font dates from 1633. One of the curates of the church was Jeremiah Horrocks, who predicted the transit of Venus and observed it from nearby Carr Howse in November 1639. A chapel to commemorate this event was added in 1859. (See also Carr House, p. 47.)

Radcliffe: Church of St. Mary's.
Off the A6053 between Bury and Bolton.

THIS church is possibly of Saxon origin, but has seen many changes through the years. The present tower was built in 1665, incorporating from an earlier building the outer doorway to the turret and battlemented parapet and the tracery of the west window. Probably the oldest complete section of the church is the nave, the arcading being built about 1400 and the clerestory some years later, the windows and those of the choir vestry being similar to those in the original south aisle. The roof which was replaced in 1870 preserved the general design of the original, the bosses being beautifully and intricately carved.

The south gable wall of the south transept probably dates from the early 15th century and was possibly part of a chantry chapel, there being an ancient piscina in the wall. The main chancel arch reputedly dates from the 13th century; other parts of the church contain some old and interesting carvings.

Rivington Parish Church.
Off A673 south of Chorley.

THERE was a church on this site as early as 1280, and a "Chapel Croft" in 1476. However, the church was not formally consecrated until 1541 at the instigation of Richard Pilkington who rebuilt it. The patronage is unusual as the inhabitants elect the minister and he is in the strange position of being chairman of his own Patrons. The original church was probably rectangular; the chancel built of local sandstone was added in 1666 and the oak beams are still to be seen. It is thought that the screen, much repaired, may have been removed from Ladyhill in Anderton before the reformation. The pulpit is oak of Tudor design from about the late 15th century.

A picture of Richard Pilkington with his family hangs on the north wall; there are also two small early 17th century brasses of the Shaw family which include in the inscription details of wills left by the respective persons. It is believed the monies recorded are still in use for an educational endowment and the Shaw's Charities. Among the modern brasses is one of particular note—an angel holding a memorial tablet. In the churchyard is a bellhouse built about 1611 to house the bell purchased by Richard Pilkington. This was found to be too heavy and large for the bellcot and probably had to be struck with a hammer—unfortunately it is no longer there.

Rufford Parish Church: St. Mary the Virgin.
Rufford is on the A59 Ormskirk to Preston road.

THE original church, which probably dated back to the early 12th century, suffered from pillaging during the Civil War and was replaced in 1736 by a simple Georgian building. In 1869 this in turn was demolished, and the present perfect example of an early Victorian church was built. Fragments of the old structure remain

—on either side of the main porch are two corbels from the principal chancel arch dated 1587. The present chancel covers the site of the two earlier ones, and incorporates some flag stones from the 18th century church. The Hesketh Chapel contains an alabaster tombstone to Thomas and Margery Hesketh and their eleven children, of 1463. On the north wall is a brass effigy of Sir Robert Hesketh dating from 1543, and many other memorials to this family are to be found in the church. The royal arms and a chandelier dated 1763 can be seen in the vestry. In the southern part of the churchyard is the base of an old preaching cross, dated 1,000 A.D. now surmounted by a sundial, and stocks removed from the old village green. (See also Rufford Old Hall, page 31).

Standish: Church of St. Wilfred.
On the A49 north of Wigan.

FIRST mentioned in 1205 and rebuilt during the years 1582–89, St. Wilfred's is one of the most interesting churches in Lancashire. It has always been noted for its bells, of which there are eight dating from 1715. The tower was part of the original building, the spire being added at a later date. The nave, aisles and chancel aisles have magnificent 17th century wooden roofs panelled in squares, the bosses being ornamented by the initials and crests of the donors. An unusual boss of a grinning ape is on the most easterly roof principal. The altar has an unusual hexagonal marble top given to the church in 1693; a legend says that the marble was cracked by Cromwell's men but dates belie this story. On the chancel floor there are several brasses, the earliest dating from about 1656.

The Duxbury Chapel, to the north of the chancel, belonged to the Standish family of Duxbury, from whom Captain Miles Standish was descended. Born in 1584, he was commissioned in the army of Elizabeth I and sailed with the Pilgrim Fathers to America in 1620. The Standish Chapel contains the oldest piece of glass in the church —the family arms dated 1584.

Before leaving the chancel notice the piers; in the north pier there is a doorway, now blocked up, which led to the Rood loft, probably above a chantry chapel. As such a chapel was abolished in 1548 it supposes that that part of the church is from the earlier building.

Also of note is the old sallet, or helmet, now on a bracket on the south pier. It is a very rare example, and probably belonged to a member of the Standish family who was knighted in 1482. The pulpit dates from 1616, and behind the prayer desk stands a gravestone dating from the 14th century and probably the oldest memorial in the church.

Stidd, near Ribchester: Church of St. Savoir.
Off B6245, turn right over the river bridge on entering Ribchester.

THIS small and ancient 13th century church stands in the middle of a field. Originally the church of the Knights Templar, it retains some of the old Norman stonework, the most notable being the now bricked up north doorway which has some fine zig-zag carving. The interior is simple with little ornamentation; the font is 15th century and the plain oak screen 17th century. An ancient stone coffin, probably the tomb of one of the Knights, can be seen in the church. (admission may be gained by obtaining the key from the Roman Museum in Ribchester.)

Not far from the gate into the churchyard stands the base of an old Norman cross. In the lane leading to the church is a most unusual building, having a long loggia with wide curving steps giving access to a group of almshouses which were built about 1728.

Upholland: Church of St. Thomas the Martyr.
On A577 Wigan to Ormskirk road.

IN 1319 a small Benedictine priory was founded at Up Holland (as it then was) with a Father Prior and twelve monks, Edward II staying for a few days within a short time of completion in 1323. The present church has been built on the chancel of the old priory which has its very fine medieval and gothic nave incorporated into the later building. Worthy of note is the wooden font, and the unusual window in the north wall made out of medieval glass found in pieces on the site. There is also some excellent modern carving on the chancel screen. In the churchyard may be seen the old village stocks.

Whalley: Church of St. Mary.
On A59 Preston to Clitheroe road.

THREE Saxon crosses in the churchyard suggest that the parish church at Whalley was in existence long before the abbey was built in 1296. The main church as it is known today dates from the 13th century and has a tower built two hundred years later. The clerestory and aisle windows, particularly the east window which has the coats of arms of famous local families, are worthy of note. Among the many treasures in the church are twenty-two 15th century canopied stalls, probably removed from the abbey and having remarkable carvings, one representing the shoeing of a goose and another St. George grappling with the dragon. More beautiful carving is seen on the screened pews of the late 17th century.

In the Soldiers' Chapel is a brass which had at some time been removed from the church and lost for a considerable period; eventually it was dug up in Garstang church and returned to Whalley. Now on a board fixed to a pillar, it shows the figure of Sir Ralph Caterall wearing armour and kneeling towards a desk. Behind him are shown his nine sons, and facing is Elizabeth, his wife, wearing a close fitting dress with fur trimmed cuffs. Behind her are arrayed her eleven daughters, in long dresses and, like their mother, wearing head dresses of the period. The brass dates from about 1515. There is also a seat for the Constable, who was held responsible for whipping noisy or restless dogs out of the church. (See also Whalley Abbey, p. 33.)

Saxon cross at Whalley.

Wigan: Church of All Saints.

THE date of the foundation of this building is uncertain, although mention was made of a church at Wigan in the Domesday Survey of 1086. Standing on a hill in the centre of the town, the present structure is probably the third on this site and largely dates from 1845–50. The lower portion of the tower, the oldest remaining part, is 13th century. The thickness of the walls suggest a fortress, and there is a massive arch opening into the church. Under the tower can be seen a 13th century window, and part of a pagan Roman altar has been preserved on the east side of the window in the north wall —it was probably used in the Roman station of Coccium which was possibly on the church site. Built into the wall of the tower is a stone slab with a foliated cross carved on it, and a similar slab is to be found by the door to the Crawford Chapel. They are probably coffin lids from the 14th century.

The two turrets on either side of the chancel arch, though much repaired, date from the 13th century. The high altar is probably 17th century, having a black stone top supported on a carved wooden frame. Behind the altar stands an elaborate reredos carved in 1847. The lofty nave contains re-used stone from the 14th century building and, with the aisles, has the original medieval roof. Near the present font stands the bowl of its 14th century predecessor, used for many years as a rain butt in the garden of the hall!

On the south side of the chancel is the Crawford Chapel, founded by Lady Mabel Bradshaigh of Haigh Hall who was the heroine of the legend of Mab's Cross. Through the years the chapel fell into decay and was rebuilt in 1719 by Sir William Bradshaigh, this structure in turn being demolished and rebuilt in 1847 by the 23rd Earl of Crawford who had inherited the chapel. The tomb of Lady Mabel and her husband is still to be seen, although the figure of Lady Mabel was re-chiselled and a new one made of Sir William, the old figure being placed in the tomb. One of the oldest parts of the church is the Walmsley Chapel, founded towards the end of the Middle Ages and probably rebuilt about 1751. Among the ancient and beautiful monuments to be found in Wigan church are two brasses. One to Susannah Shaw is badly worn, but is dated 1685; the other is to Albert Hodd, a curate of the church who died in 1876, and is unusual for it shows a priest in eucharistic vestments. (See Legend of Mab's Cross, p. 15; Haigh Hall, p. 35.)

Woodplumpton Church.

Woodplumpton: Church of St. Anne.
On B5411 north-west of Preston.

THIS attractive church, built of deep cream coloured stone, is worth a visit if motoring nearby. Beside the lychgate are the old stocks, while a mounting block built into the wall is a reminder of the days when worshippers came on horse-back. On entering the church the stone arches and low ceilings create an immediate impression of unusual charm, the three aisles each having a separate roof. The north wall shows signs of having been part of a very early church, probably 12th century, although restorations took place in 1639 and 1748. There is an old bell dated 1596, now mounted for preservation, and a Jacobean Holy Table, dated 1635. Surmounting the octagonal bell tower is an unusual weather-vane in the shape of a sea-horse. Down the main path in the churchyard is a large boulder said to mark the site of the grave of Meg Shelton, the reputed witch. (See Ghosts and Witches, Meg Shelton, p. 16.)

6: Museums and Art Galleries

Haworth Art Gallery, Haworth Park, Accrington.
On A679 Burnley to Blackburn road. Open daily: 2 p.m.–5 p.m. Sundays, 6 *p.m.*-8 *p.m.*

THIS beautiful house standing in the grounds of Haworth Park was built in 1909 through the generosity of Mr. William Haworth and his sister Anne, who were well known Accrington cotton manufacturers. There is a collection of 18th–20th century oil paintings and a large collection of early English water colours including works by Sandby, Cox, Birkett and Hunt. Of great interest to visiting Americans is the largest display of Tiffany Favrile glassware anywhere in Europe—over 100 pieces including vases, tiles and mosaics. Much of the glass was given to the museum by a Mr. Briggs, an Accrington man who worked for Louis Comfort Tiffany in America. Loan exhibitions by the Arts Council and the Victoria and Albert Museum are staged here between April and October, together with temporary exhibitions by northern artists.

Bacup Natural History Society Museum, 24 Yorkshire Street, Bacup.
Route: A671 Burnley to Rochdale road. Open by appointment only.

THIS museum was founded in the late 19th century, and has an interesting collection of items built up through the years by working naturalists. Exhibitions are varied and include a collection of domestic bygones as well as items of local interest to show the social history of the area. There is a good collection of archaeological material including Neolithic flint, arrow heads, scrapers and adze heads, and of special interest is the display of different minerals and geological findings. For many years the society has maintained a strong tradition of geological interest and much of the museum's collection has been supplied by members working in local pits which are now closed.

The museum is run by officers of the society; written application for a visit should be made to the president of the society at the museum address.

Lewis Textile Museum, Exchange Street, Blackburn.
Open: Monday to Saturday, 10 a.m.–5 p.m. Wednesday and Friday, open until 7.30 p.m.

A SMALL but most interesting collection of domestic and industrial items is housed here. The great inventors of the industrial revolution came from Lancashire: John Kay from Bury, James Hargreaves from Stanhill, Richard Arkwright from Preston and Samuel Crompton from Bolton. The Lewis Museum shows their inventions and how they changed the pattern of weaving and spinning from one of cottage labour to organised factory work. There are full scale replicas of Hargreaves' spinning jenny of 1764, Richard Arkwright's spinning-frame of 1770, Kay's fly shuttle of 1733 and Crompton's mule of 1779. Three rooms depict typical homes at different stages of the industrial revolution. An early cottage shows a man weaving and two women spinning. A yeoman's house of 17th century period with 18th century furniture has two women with spinning wheels making linen thread. The replica of the gentleman's drawing-room is of the late 18th century and shows ladies spinning for pleasure. A typical Lancashire loom developed during the 19th century from an earlier power loom invented by Edmund Cartwright in 1786 is also on display.

Reflectaire Museum, Blackpool Airport.
Open daily 9-30 *a.m.–*6 *p.m., including Sunday Admission: Adults* 20 *p., children* 10*p. Car parking; shop; refreshments available at the airport.*

ORGANISED and arranged by an enthusiastic company, this collection transports the visitor back to World War II. It is a living museum, and not just a collection of aircraft, trucks and army vehicles.

Many static displays have been arranged including the re-construction of a war-time operations room, models depicting famous battles and a large photographic collection. The art gallery exhibits aeronautical works of established and unknown artists, and in the private cinema films about aircraft and the war are shown. The comprehensive reference library is open by appointment only. The aircraft on show are a Canadian Sabre 4, Supermarine Seafire, Chancevought Corsair, Percival Mew Gull, F.A.330 and an Avro Lancaster Bomber. This bomber has close connections with the famous 617 Dam Buster Squadron, and is never airborne unless a member of the squadron is among the crew. Service vehicles, which form a major part of the museum, include a Bren Gun Carrier, Armoured Car, Guy Gun Carrier, Jeeps, American Dodge 15 cwt. Command Car and a 13 cwt. Bedford Crew Truck. A Japanese 45 m.m. gun and a large collection of Aircraft parts are also on display.

A preservation society has been formed for all those who are interested in these aircraft and vehicles, and enquiries should be made to the director at the museum. Reflectaire, the only museum in the country dealing with aircraft of this period, is recommended to any visitor to Lancashire.

Barry Elder Doll Museum, Carr Howse, Bretherton.
On the B5247, just off the A59 Preston to Southport road. Open daily, including Sunday, 10 a.m.–8 p.m. Admission, adults 15 p, children half price. Car park; refreshments.

CARR HOWSE, a Tudor farmhouse built in 1613, houses a unique and fascinating collection of 1,200 dolls from all parts of the world, and is well worth a visit. The oldest doll is 300 years old, the youngest 50 years, the tallest four feet and the smallest less than half an inch. Many of the dolls are displayed in period settings with furniture made for them a century ago, including four-poster beds, push chairs, perambulators and rocking cradles, all of which are serviceable today. There are period doll's houses and many other toys over a hundred years old. Collections of Georgian and Victorian furniture, musical instruments, china, brass and copper are also on

Carr Howse.

display. Carr Howse is set in gardens containing 1,500 rose trees and many other interesting plants and shrubs. It was from here that Jeremiah Horrocks, the astronomer predicted and observed the transit of Venus over the sun in November 1639. (See Hoole Church, page 38).

Bury Art Gallery and Museum, Moss Street, Bury.
Open: Monday to Friday, 10 a.m.–6 p.m.; Saturday, 10 a.m.–5 p.m.; closed on Sunday.

TWO displays of weapons are housed in this small but forward-looking museum as well as a collection of historical items, mainly of local archaeological interest, and a display of British and foreign birds. The art gallery in the same building contains the Wrigley collection including 19th century paintings and engravings by Reynolds, Turner, Cox and Constable. There is also a permanent collection of works by modern artists which includes exhibits by Lowry, Epstein and Pasmere. From time to time the Victoria and Albert Museum circulation department and the North Western Museum and Art Gallery Service display works not often seen in local museums and art galleries. Further information on displays can be had by writing to the Borough Librarian and Curator at the art gallery.

Royal Umpire Museum and Carriage Exhibition, Croston.
*On the A*581 *Chorley to Southport road. Open daily, 9 a.m. to dusk, March to November. Admission: adults* 15 *p, children 5 p. Car park; restaurant.*

SOMETHING for every member of the family is to be found in this unusual museum, named after a famous stage coach which is included among the sixty on display. The visitor can see the haunted house of the Gradwells which has a priest's hiding place, and the reconstruction of a baronial hall which contains relics of the Old Croston Hall. There is an 18th century village street, built under cover, complete with shops, houses, a tavern and a coaching house. A number of small wooden buildings depict a Scottish croft, a Welsh miner's cottage, an Irish moorland cottage and an English woodman's cottage. A large "Western Town" has been built with saloon, sheriff's office, gaol and many other buildings. Nearby may be seen an exhibition of old fashioned methods of punishment including a hangman's scaffold, stocks and guillotine. For the very young a few miniature scenes have been built of farms, towns and villages and red indians. There is also a small aviary and some domestic animals in a pets' corner. Facilities are available for picnicing and deck chairs can be obtained free of charge.

A Landau at the Royal Umpire Museum, Croston.

The Higher Mill Industrial Museum, Helmshore, Rossendale.
Route: B6235 off Holcombe Road, Helmshore. Look for signpost near large stone mill; turn off main road and turn left under arch. The museum is directly ahead. Prior arrangements to visit the museum **must** *be made with the curator.*

HIGHER MILL, Helmshore, was built in 1789 and is now being restored by a charitable trust for use as an industrial museum. The mill has been scheduled as an ancient monument, and the surrounding area is of great historical importance. The nearby workers' cottages and the mill master's mansion are virtually unchanged since the 18th century. Inside the mill there is a twenty-foot waterwheel and a set of fulling and finishing machines which can be demonstrated to visitors by the curator. A list of rules which were observed on the premises can now be seen at the Lewis Textile Museum at Blackburn (see page 46). Eventually two steam engines and some of the earliest examples of textile machinery will be on view; these will include spinning jennies, hand looms and machines built by Sir Richard Arkwright, all of them being in working order. One of the last surviving beam engines is being sent by Bury Corporation, there are also plans to restore the mill master's mansion and the cottages which will be furnished in period style. Visitors can tour the extensive grounds, woods and reservoirs.

At Helmshore Station the East Lancashire Railway Preservation

Society has opened a museum and is hoping to purchase a length of railway line between Stubbins Junction and Grane Road, Haslingden.

Lytham Motive Power Museum.
Route: Off the A584 Preston to Blackpool road; turn left at traffic lights on entering Lytham. Open: At Easter and Whitsun, then from first weekend in June, daily except Monday and Friday, 11 a.m.–6 p.m. Admission: adults 15 p, children 6 p.

THE oldest engine in the museum dates from 1887 and is on display with nine other engines of varying ages, all housed under one roof. There is also a large model railway lay-out. Outside two engines take it in turns to pull a small train round the yards, where other rolling stock may be seen. This track is one foot ten and three-quarter inches gauge, the charge being 5p per ride.

Harris Museum and Art Gallery, Market Square, Preston.
Open every day, 10 a.m.–6 p.m.

THIS building, designed by James Hibbert, a Preston man, is said to be one of the finest examples of academic architecture in this country. It was made possible by the bequest of Edmund Robert Harris, also of Preston, and opened by the Earl of Derby in October 1893. The plan has been developed round a great central hall, rising the full height of the building and expressed externally in a tall square lantern. Within this lantern is housed the famous Foucault Pendulum, 115 feet long with a bob weighing 30 lbs. indicating the movement of the earth on its own axis. After entering through a central portico, notice the inlaid marble floor with staircases rising on either side to the galleried floors above and emphasised by Greek friezes copied from the Parthenon and the Temple of Apollo Epicurus. Externally much precise neo-Greek detail will be noticed, following the style of continental architecture of the day.

The museum and art gallery contain many 19th and 20th century paintings, notable displays of English pottery, porcelain and enamels, a magnificent collection of costumes and accessories of the 18th and 19th centuries, also Victoriana and scent bottles. To interest girls there are dressed dolls and miniature objects, while for their brothers there are birds eggs, coins and medals. Remains from the Bleasdale Circle are also on display. The library contains rare and valuable early printed books, and is mainly of antiquarian interest. (See Bleasdale Circle, p. 21.)

Whitaker Park Museum and Art Gallery, Whitaker Park, Rawtenstall.
A56 Bury to Burnley road. Open: April to September, weekdays 2 p.m.–5 p.m., 6 p.m.–8 p.m. or dusk; Saturday 10 a.m.–12 noon; Sunday 3 p.m.–5 p.m. October to March, weekdays 2 p.m.–5 p.m.; Saturday 10 a.m.–12 noon; closed Sunday.

THE museum was formed in 1901 as part of a gift to the borough by Mr. Richard Whitaker, a native of Rawtenstall who had risen to wealth from a poor childhood. The museum presents two exhibitions, one of temporary displays and a permanent exhibition known as the Rossendale collection. This concentrates on showing different aspects of the local life and history of the area, and is most interesting. Paintings and photographs depict scenes from the late 17th century to recent times, and there are many items to show the domestic and industrial history of the district. A display of clog making is of particular interest. The skilled clog maker was a well known figure in yesterday's Lancashire, and many people will still remember his shop, with its rows of wooden soles and heavy irons. Today the craft is rare, and the shops where one can still buy a warm and comfortable clog to fit are few and far between. The museum shows the tools used in shaping clogs, with wooden blocks at different stages of shaping and a selection of irons. There are examples of clog uppers and several finished clogs of various types.

Also in the Rossendale collection is a display of toll boards showing the tolls exacted for travellers and their animals on some of the old Lancashire turnpike roads. In the second half of the 18th century new roads were made and governed by turnpike trusts, who charged a toll on all travellers using them. Amounts varied from road to road and were always advertised on special toll boards—those on display here show a table of weights for the Burnley and Edenfield turnpike roads, a table of tolls for the Newhallhey Bridge toll bar and a water bar for the Haslingden and Todmorden road. The museum also has an exhibition of porcelain and furniture, as well as the Peer-Groves collection of pottery and English table glass.

Botanic Gardens Museum, Churchtown, Southport.
Off the A565 Preston to Southport road. Open, May to September, weekdays 10 a.m.–6 p.m.; Sundays 2 p.m.–5 p.m. October to April, weekdays 10 a.m.–5 p.m.; Sundays 2 p.m.–5 p.m.

IN the 19th century Churchtown was famous for its strawberry gardens, and attracted many visitors who came to see—and sample—the fruits. In 1874 they were leased by a private company and the land was landscaped for use as a pleasure garden. The first museum was opened in 1876 and for many years showed curiosities and viewing machines for the public's entertainment. In 1936 this building and most of the gardens were bought by the Corporation of Southport, the present museum being opened in 1938. It specialises in presenting displays of local interest, the natural history and botanical sections being extremely good. There is a fine collection of mounted birds, most of which are local, and a particularly good specimen of the golden eagle. There are different types of sea shells and a display of butterflies. The botanical collection is of special interest, with over 300 detailed water colour paintings of wild flowers and grasses. These are grouped according to the time of year when they appear in the countryside.

In the local history room paintings and photographs show the development of Southport from the mid-19th century, with some ivory models of some of the town's earliest buildings. The Victorian period room shows furniture, costumes and bygones of the last century. Not to be missed is the old fire engine, which in the mid-19th century was stationed at Scarisbrick Hall and was manned by volunteers. The museum also presents travelling exhibitions loaned from the Victoria and Albert Museum in London.

Art Gallery and Museum, Station Road, Wigan.

THESE new premises opened in April 1968 are situated in the Powell Building, Station Road, and contain material relating to the history and former industries of the town. The art gallery holds many visiting exhibitions, including paintings and other visual arts from the Victoria and Albert Museum, the North West Museum and Art Gallery Service, the Arts Council, and the Art Exhibitions Bureau. The museum holds a permanent display of local history exhibits. These include Roman coins discovered in Wigan in 1925, Stone Age implements, pewter, pottery, antique guns and pistols. Examples of Wigan's industries include cannel coal, bell-founding and watch-making.

7: Nature Reserves and Bird Sanctuaries

FOR those readers who are interested in nature reserves and the preservation of all types of wild life, details of as many reserves as possible have been included. The wardens and those in charge stress the necessity for extreme care when visiting the reserves, and ask for the help of visitors in preserving the many rare and valuable species that may be seen.

Ainsdale Sand Dunes National Nature Reserve.
Off A565 north of Formby.

SITUATED between Southport and Formby, this reserve covers 1,216 acres of sand-dunes. Apart from the more common plants and birds to be seen, many species which are being lost due to excessive collecting are being encouraged to return. The reserve is noted for its sand lizards and natterjack toads, and red squirrels are to be found in the pine woods on the east fringe. It is also internationally famous for its calcareous (limestone bearing) sand-dunes and plants which are particular to this region. The three-quarters of a mile long Fisherman's Path is the most direct route to the shore and is particularly interesting because it shows all the main ecological features of the area. Immediately to the north is the educational zone, used by teachers and school-children for field studies. From the highest point on the dunes there is a magnificent view of the reserve and the south-west coast line of Lancashire.

No permit is needed to use the clearly marked public footpath through the reserve, but a map must first be obtained from the office. A souvenir guide, "Ainsdale Wild Life", is also available. Great care should be taken at all times to observe all the conditions set out by the Conservancy. Dogs are allowed, but must be kept on a lead. Further information is obtainable from The Naturalist Warden, 18, Brows Lane, Formby, telephone Formby 3019.

Borsdane Wood Bird Sanctuary, Hindley.
Hindley lies between A58 and A577 south-east of Wigan.

THIS small reserve in a wood of oak, beech, sycamore and horse-chestnut is about one mile long. In the last ten years over 90 species of birds have been recorded, including tawny owls, great spotted woodpeckers, tree creepers, blackcaps, jays and kestrels. Many other common woodland species have nested in the area. During the last few years an extensive programme for ringing many blue, great, coal and willow tits has been carried out.

Lytham St. Annes Nature Reserve.

OCCUPYING an area of about 39 acres, this reserve lies to the east of the A584 St. Annes to Blackpool road on sand-dunes which are easily accessible. There is a local warden in attendance to point out the many varieties of butterflies and moths and the interesting types of flora on the reserve, some being quite rare specimens. Birds such as kestrels, stonechats, goldfinches, linnets, warblers, gulls and mallards are often to be seen in a natural habitat.

Southport Bird Sanctuary.

THE sanctuary adjoins the Ainsdale Reserve to the north, and has been established to protect the roosts of wintering geese, duck and waders. Access is unrestricted.

A natterjack toad.

8: Docks and Waterways

Canal Cruising: The Lancaster Canal.

THE Lancaster Canal, which originally ran between Kendal and Wigan, was opened in June 1819. It was planned to be carried over the Ribble estuary at Preston on a massive aqueduct, but the cost of this proved to be prohibitive and the two sections were joined by a tramway. In 1879 the tramway was closed; the canal was thus left in two halves and the southern portion fell into disuse. On the Kendal to Preston section a daily passenger service was started in 1820, covering the 57 miles in 14 hours, and in 1833 an express boat was introduced which cut this time to seven and a half hours. The passenger boats were finally withdrawn in 1849. The Lancaster Canal now runs for 42 miles from Tewitfields north of Carnforth to Preston with a branch off to Glasson Dock.

Today the boats on the canal are used for pleasure purposes; many are privately owned but there are a number of passenger cruisers:

1. Adventure Cruisers, Jolly Roger Boating Haven, Catforth, near Preston. Telephone 077-474 232. Take the B5269 from Broughton for 1¾ miles, turn left to Catforth and after 1½ miles turn left at a T-junction, from where it is half a mile to Swillbrook Bridge and the boat yard.
2. Kenneth A. Preston, 4 Beech Avenue, Warton, near Preston. Telephone Freckleton 823. Moorings are at Moon Bridge Wharf, Hollowfirth Lane, Woodplumpton. North from Preston turn left at Broughton on to B5269 and continue for 1½ miles to a T-junction. Here turn right towards Barton, a journey of a quarter mile bringing you to Moons Wharf.

Hirings for the week and, according to availability, for the day or weekend may be had from both these firms, prices ranging from £16 to £42 according to size and season. Day bookings and charges will be given on request from the firms concerned. From Preston a pleasure cruiser, the *Shelagh*, sails every Sunday from the end of June onwards. Further details may be obtained by writing to D. Ashcroft, Esq., 12 Staveley Place, Preston.

The Lancaster Canal Trust is an organisation which, while engaged on projects to improve the canal, also arranges private cruises for its members. Membership of the Trust is 50p. for adults; 25 p. for juniors; 75p. for a family. Further details may be obtained by writing to the Public Relations Officer, 16 Cranbourne Avenue, Church, Accrington.

Canal Cruising: The Leeds and Liverpool Canal.

THIS canal which winds its way through the central and southern parts of Lancashire is said to be one of the finest in the country, and has been described as "interesting, dramatic, magnificent and defying description". It is therefore surely a "must" for those with an interest in cruising. Boats are available at various points along the canal, those in central Lancashire being:

1. Canal Boats Ltd., The Ship Inn, Haskayne, near Ormskirk, just off A567 Liverpool to Southport road. Telephone Halsall 446.
2. Summit Holidays Afloat, Finsley Gate Marina, Burnley. Telephone Padiham 71175.

Both these yards have cruisers for hire, with prices ranging from £10 to £70 per week according to size (two to six berth) and season (March to early October). Canal Boats Ltd. also hire cruisers for day or weekend cruises according to availability. For furher information please contact the firms director.

Information on both the Leeds and Liverpool and Lancaster canals may be obtained by writing to British Waterways Board, Melbury House, Melbury Terrace, London, N.W.1.

Fleetwood: Fishing port, docks and harbour.
On A587 north of Blackpool. The fish dock is closed at the weekend.

SITUATED on the estuary of the river Wyre, Fleetwood is a natural port and sheltered harbour having two enclosed docks—the **Wyre Dock** and **Fish Dock.** It is marked out by its geographical position as the fishing industry's "gateway to the west" and is an ideal centre for the delivery of fish to the inland markets. Fleetwood has thus become the third largest fishing port in England and the foremost on the western sea-board. It is the premier port for the landing of hake, although cod, haddock, plaice, sole, skate, roker, cole, bream, ling, pollack, gurnet, whiting, herring and mackerel are also landed in season. Altogether some 900,000 cwts of fish are handled annually.

In the past 16 years the trawler owners have modernised the fleet by replacing coal-burning vessels with modern diesel ships, and installing the latest developments in electronic equipment for navigation and fish finding. Near water trawlers, 80ft. to 110 ft., and middle water trawlers, 110ft. to 140ft., fish as far as the coasts of Holland,

A Fleetwood trawler.

Denmark and the southern tip of Norway, the North Sea, Dogger Bank, Irish Sea and the coasts of Ireland and Scotland as far north as the Faroe Islands. Distant water trawlers, over 140ft. long, have fishing grounds 2,000 to 4,000 miles away in Newfoundland, west and southern Greenland, Bear Island, the Barents and White Seas to the north of Russia, and the western Norwegian coast. Freezer and factory trawlers, 200ft. in length, stay up to 60 days at sea, the fish is frozen whole into large blocks or sometimes skinned by machine, filleted and frozen. In addition to the deep sea trawlers, there are some 40 to 50 inshore fishing vessels operating from the port, each with a crew of two to four men.

Some fish is auctioned at the docks, being bought by coastal merchants and frozen food firms. Speed of distribution is essential, and Fleetwood was the first fishing port to launch its own road distribution service loading directly from the docks into insulated containers. The modern ice factory at the port can produce 500 tons of ice per day, which can be loaded by hopper into the holds of the trawlers. The public are allowed to walk round the fish sheds which surround the dock. The greatest activity is in the early part of the week during the mornings; it is suggested that on such a visit strong shoes should be worn as the dock is wet and slippery.

Wyre Dock deals with dry bulk and liquid goods, including chemicals, sand and gravel. Cranes, transit sheds, dock road and railway systems can be seen here, vessels being able to load to or from road and rail vehicles simultaneously.

Further information can be obtained from the Secretary, Fleetwood Fishing Vessel Owners Association, Dock Street, Fleetwood, Lancs.

Port of Preston.
Main entrance is Dock Road, off the A583 Preston to Blackpool road.

SITUATED on the river Ribble, Preston docks were started in 1892 and are well worth a visit. The Ionic and Bardic ferries sail regularly to Ireland, and banana boats from the West Indies can frequently be seen plying down the Ribble. Other vessels annually bring well over 2 million tons of cargo from all over the world, including wood pulp, citrus fruit, ore, paper, china clay, iron and steel and timber. At the time of writing Preston has the reputation of being the second largest container handling port in the British Isles.

Goods are landed direct from the ship to rail, road vehicles, or to the warehouses, there being 18 electric cranes, 23 mobile steam, diesel and petrol electric cranes, 4 fork-lift trucks and a fleet of mobile tractors and trailers for all kinds of timber. There are two coaling hoists for coal and coke. Roll-on-roll-off loading ramps have been provided for the expanding road traffic to Ireland. Storage tanks for one million gallons of petroleum and other oil products are also situated here. The Ribble branch railway connects direct from the docks to the main line system at Preston.

For further information and permission to see the docks contact the General Manager, Dock Offices, Preston.

9: Sports and Hobbies

IN this section it has only been possible to give the names and addresses of a few of the more specialised clubs. Those requiring information on other clubs and societies in local areas should apply to their Town Hall or Public Library where a comprehensive list will be found.

Angling

IT is usually possible to obtain day tickets to fish from the many piers that abound on the Lancashire coast line. For those who prefer a more specialised type of angling it is often possible to obtain day tickets or weekly permits to fish in one of the rivers or reservoirs. As the names and addresses of local secretaries are liable to change, those interested should obtain a complete and up to date list from the Lancashire River Authority, 48 West Cliff, Preston, telephone number Preston 54921.

Archery.

ORIGINALLY a means of hunting and war, archery has been considered a sport for many hundreds of years. The Royal Company of Archers was founded in 1676. In Lancashire there are many archery clubs both for field and target archery, the oldest club dating back to 1902. This is the Bowmen of Pendle and Samlesbury who shoot in the grounds of Samlesbury Hall. Other clubs include the Blackpool Bowmen, Billinge Bowmen (near Wigan), the Bowmen of Overdale, the Grange and Allithwaite Archers, Mersey Bowmen, Preston Archers and the Walverden Bowmen. Further information may be obtained by writing to the Secretary of the Grand National Archery Society, 20, Broomfield Road, Chelmsford, Essex.

Canoeing.

THERE are a number of local canoe clubs in Lancashire affiliated to the British Canoe Union, these including the Manchester Canoe Club, the Grappenhall Athletic Canoe Club, the Lakeland

Canoe Club and the Canoe Camping Club. Membership of the B.C.U. is 75p per year for a full member, and further details may be obtained from the General Secretary, British Canoe Union, 26/29 Park Crescent, London, W.1. The canoe clubs in Lancashire arrange many events, both inside and outside the county, and these include slaloms, sea surfing, cruises, regattas and wild water races. Meetings are held on stretches of the Dee, Lune, Ribble, Wharfe and other Pennine rivers.

Folk Dancing.

THE English Folk Dance and Song Society (North Lancashire District) both organise and take part in many interesting events throughout the county. These include barn dances, folk dance parties and social events during the winter months, and displays at carnivals and processions during the summer. The Leyland Morris Men undertake evening tours of the local towns and villages, sometimes accompanied by the Furness Morris Men and the Hoghton Rapper Sword Team. The Manchester Morris Men specialise in the traditional clog processional dances of this region. Further details of the many local clubs and events may be obtained by writing to the Area Organiser, 4 Bluecoat Chambers, School Lane, Liverpool 1.

British Gliding Association.

LANCASHIRE has two gliding clubs, and newcomers to this sport may go along any Saturday or Sunday and introduce themselves. If under 21 they will have to have their parents' written permission before the club will take them up on an air experience flight. Holiday courses are run by the Lakes Gliding Club at Walney Island from June to August and cost about £26—this includes bunkhouse accommodation, all meals and approximately 20 flights. Families, providing the children are over the age of 16, are accepted, and bookings are weekly from Friday to Saturday. The addresses of the two Lancashire Clubs are: The Blackpool and Fylde Gliding Club, Blackpool Airport, Blackpool. Telephone: 41526. Lakes Gliding Club, Walney Airfield, Barrow-in-Furness. Telephone 41458.

Go-karting.

THE Lancashire Kart Club organise monthly meetings at Burtonwood, near Warrington, throughout the year. Membership of the club is £1.50 per year, and for juniors 75p. The club is R.A.C. approved, and members can compete at any R.A.C. circuit in the U.K. or in any international event held abroad. Other clubs in

Lancashire include the Ribble Kart Club which meets at Flookburgh (near Grange-over-Sands); the Morecambe and Heysham Kart Club which meets at Heysham Head; and the Lion Kart Club which organises events at Tern Hill.

Ski-ing.

For those interested in ski-ing, a ski club is held on Pendle Hill and ski lessons are also given. All enquiries should be made to the headquarters at the Well Springs Hotel, Nick o' Pendle, Sabden. Also of interest is the Preston Dry Ski School; further information may be obtained c/o Preston Sports Depot, Friargate, Preston.

Sub Aqua Clubs.

THE British Sub Aqua Club has many local branches throughout Lancashire, the addresses of which can be obtained from the headquarters of the club at 25 Orchard Road, Kingston-upon-Thames, Surrey. Inland as well as coastal towns are represented and, although most of the diving is done in the sea and lakes, many clubs have "practice nights" at their local swimming baths. Included among the activities of sub aqua enthusiasts are such programmes as: (a) underwater surveys for different biological, archaeological and fishing societies; (b) searches for sunken boats and wrecks; (c) lobster and crab fishing. Organised parties of B.S.A.C. members travel to diving locations in various parts of the British Isles.

Vintage Cars.

THERE is a growing interest in Lancashire in vintage cars, and many events are held which are of widespread interest. The Preston and District Vintage Car Club was founded in 1959, and organises frequent rallies during the summer months, social events during the winter and an annual static exhibition of vintage cars at Loxhams Garage in Preston in April. It is associated with the Manchester Vintage Car Club and publishes its own monthly bulletin, *The Klaxon*, containing details of all the events held in the north-west area. Further information about the club may be obtained from the Secretary, Woodfield House, Woodplumpton, near Preston.

Yachting.

Affiliated Member Clubs of the Royal Yachting Association:

Locality	*Club*
Blackpool Stanley Park Lake.	Blackpool Light Craft Club.
Bolton Belmont Reservoir.	Bolton S. C.
Bolton Delph Reservoir.	Delph S. C.
Clowbridge Reservoir.	Rossendale Valley S. C.
Colne.	University of Bradford Union S. C.
Elton Reservoir Bury.	Elton S. C.
Foulridge, Nr. Colne.	Burwain S. C.
Littleborough, Nr. Rochdale.	Hollingworth Lake, S. C.
Lytham.	Lytham Y. C.
Ribble Estuary, Lytham.	Ribble Cruising Club.
Poolstock (Scotsman's Flash).	Wigan S. C.
Rishton Reservoir, Nr. Blackburn.	East Lancashire S. C.

10: Events

JANUARY

Bolton:
A New Year's Day Dog Show is held in the Drill Hall, Silverwell Street, Bolton.

Ramsbottom:
The Old English Game Fowl Society Show is held on New Year's Day at the Rose and Crown Hotel, Carr Street, Ramsbottom.

APRIL

Bacup:
The Britannia Coconut Dancers perform two dances on Easter Saturday each year. Dressed in black and white, wearing clogs and with their faces blackened, they dance through the streets of Bacup.
Blackpool$_5$ A brass band Contest is held on the south pier, bands from Lancashire and the surrounding counties competing.

Bolton:
A summer season of plays are performed at the Octagan Theatre from the beginning of April to the end of June. The box office opens 10.30 a.m. to 6 p.m.

Holcombe Hunt Point-to-Point: Held at the traditional course at Nab Gate, Harwood, near Bolton. The kennels are at Kirklees, Tottington.

Pendle Forest and Craven Harriers Hunt Point-to-Point: Held at Sawley, near Clitheroe.

Preston:
Pace Egging in Avenham Park, Preston, takes place on Easter Monday. The custom dates back to about 1290. The children celebrate by rolling hard boiled eggs down the slopes.

Rivington:
A fair is held annually at the top of Rivington Pike at Easter; there is also a race from Lever Park to the top of the Pike and down again.

MAY

Blackpool:

A seven-a-side Rugby League knock-out competition takes place at the Blackpool Borough Rugby League ground.

The Royal Lancashire Agricultural Society's Spring Show is held at East Park Drive, Blackpool.

The Tower Circus summer season opens during May, performing once nightly at 7.15 p.m. with certain matinees. From the beginning of June onwards there are two performances daily at 2.15 p.m. and 7.15 p.m. Prices for adults range from 75p. to 35p. and for children from 40p. to 20p. The circus is housed beneath one of Lancashire's most famous landmarks, Blackpool Tower. It is possible to take one of two lifts to "The Crow's Nest," almost at the top of the Tower from where views of the Lake District hills and the Isle of Man can be seen. Also in the Tower building is an excellent aquarium with many sea water and tropical fish.

Clitheroe:

During the Mayor-making ceremonies members of the Council walk in procession. The Town Sergeant in red robes, and ringing a bell, visits each school declaring a holiday. (See Clitheroe Castle, p. 26.)

Todmorden:

A carnival is held in the town with a procession from Halifax Road to Centre Vale Park where a carnival queen is crowned. It is hoped that future carnival events will last for a week.

JUNE

Accrington:

The East Lancashire group of advanced motorists hold their annual manoeuvreability and road tests on the Broadway Car Park.

Blackpool:

The three-day Blackpool Annual Championship Dog Show is held at the Oval, Stanley Park. Admission is 25p.

Highland Games also take place at the Oval. Prices of admission are 15p. for adults and 7½p. for children.

Burnley:

The one-day Burnley Agricultural Society Show takes place.

Bury:

The one-day Bury and District Agricultural Society Show is put on at Broad Oak Farm, Fairfield, Bury.

Lytham:

A procession of floats, dancers and bands walks through the streets on Club Day; during the afternoon the Rose Queen is crowned in nearby Lowther Gardens. (Many of the towns and villages in Lancashire hold carnival or club days, but as Lytham is one of the oldest it merits special mention.)

Manchester to Blackpool Walk:
A road race attracting a large number of walkers.
Manchester to Blackpool veteran and vintage car run:
This very popular event finishes with a rally at Stanley Park, Blackpool.
Preston:
On a Saturday in mid-June a children's dance festival is held at Avenham Park, children from a large number of schools and clubs taking part. This is a feature of the summer programme of the English Folk Dance and Song Society (see page 60).
River Ribble at Lytham:
A sailing regatta on the river attracts craft from many parts of Lancashire.
Southport:
A one-day horse and dog show is held at the Victoria Park. The showground opens at 8.30 a.m. and the admission charges are 37½p. for adults and 17½p. for children.
Stoneyhurst College:
The College is open to the public for the procession of the Blessed Sacrament on the feast of Corpus Christi (tenth day after Whit Sunday). Ancient vestments only used on this day can be seen as the pupils and priests walk in solemn procession.
Todmorden:
The one-day Todmorden Agricultural Society Show takes pace.

JULY

Blackburn:
The two-day Blackburn Agricultural Society Show is held in Witton Park. Admission prices are: Day 1, adults 20p., children 10p. Day 2, adults 25p., children 15p.
Blackpool:
The Royal Lancashire Agricultural Society Show at East Park Drive is a three-day event, admission prices vary according to day and time. They range from £1 on the first day to 50p. on the third day, prices being reduced after 3 p.m. The admission price for children is 20p. In 1972, Guild Year, the show will be held in Preston, and subsequently at the new permanent showground at Ribby Corner, Wrea Green, near Kirkham.
Bolton:
The autumn season of plays at the Octagan Theatre, Bolton commences at the end of July. The booking office is open 10.30 a.m. to 6 p.m.
Bury:
A Festival of Sport lasts for a week, and includes angling, bowling, soccer, cycling, athletics and swimming.

Fleetwood to Morecambe Swim:
This event is organised by the Morecambe Cross-Bay Swimming Association.

Goosnargh:
Everybody's Dog Show is held at Chingle Hall, Goosnargh. Admission prices are: Adults 15p., children 7½p. The hall is open to the public (for details see Ghosts, Witches and Legends, page 14).

Preston to Morecambe carnival run:
For veteran, vintage and post vintage cars. The cars leave Preston during the morning, arriving at Sandylands Promenade, Morecambe at approximately mid-day. There is a simple driving test at the finishing point, while the judging of the Concours d'Elegance takes place prior to the Grand Parade during the afternoon. The run is usually held on the second Sunday in July.

Rossendale:
The annual pilgrimage to Waugh's Well in the heart of the Forest of Rossendale is held in the middle of July. It begins at Waterfoot and after a climb up to the moors, songs and poems by Edwin Waugh are sung and recited round the Well.

Southport:
The Southport Chess Festival takes place at the Cambridge Hall, the event continuing for two weeks. Play for the open championship is held each day, as well as lightning chess and simultaneous displays.

AUGUST

Blackpool:
A four-day festival of swimming is to be held each year from 1972 at the Derby Baths. This will include age group competitions, swimming and diving and team competitions. It is hoped that two water polo national championship finals may also be featured.

Claughton:
A clay-pigeon shoot takes place annually at Brock Cottage Farm, Claughton-on-Brock, near Preston.

Fleetwood:
The open international radio-controlled model power-boat regatta is held at the Marine Lake. This is organised by the Fleetwood Model Yacht and Power Boat Racing Club in conjunction with Fleetwood Corporation.

Lytham:
The Lancashire and Cheshire Budgerigar Society has a two-day show in the Lowther Pavilion.

Preston:
A Pot Fair takes place in the market place for one week, usually during the latter part of August. One of the oldest fairs in the country, it attracts many visitors.

Southport:

Southport Flower Show is held at the Victoria Park. This is a three-day show and is famous not only in Lancashire but throughout the country for its beautiful horticultural exhibits. The show includes horse jumping, and band concerts are held each day in the bandstand. Admission prices vary according to day and time, and range from £1 on the first day to 40p. on the third day. Children under the age of 15 are admitted at half price.

SEPTEMBER

Blackpool:

Blackpool Illuminations are held during September and October when fairy lights and tableaux illuminate the length of the promenade. There is no admission charge. Similar illuminations are put on at Morecambe.

The Bleasdale Beagles:

The only pack of beagles in Lancashire meets every Saturday from September to mid-March. Meets are held at Abbeystead, Trough of Bowland, Claughton-on-Brock, Chipping and many other places.

Cliviger:

The Lonk Sheep Fair usually takes place on the nearest Saturday to September 29th. The sheep dog trials commence at 8.00 a.m. and finish at approximately 7.00 p.m. Entries are limited to 80 and this is considered to be one of the best competitions in the north with competitors from many northern counties taking part. Incorporated in this event is a fell race to Thieveley Pike during the afternoon, which attracts athletes from clubs all over Britain. Admission is 10p. for adults and 2½p. for children. Car park is 5p.; refreshments are available.

Preston:

Preston Guild is held every twenty years, the next Guild being in 1972 during the last week in August or early September. On three successive market days before the celebrations there is a Proclamation by the town crier, in full ceremonial dress, in the market place at noon. The festivities begin with a parade of floats, and processions are held every day for different causes. There are dances, displays of all kinds, fireworks and exhibitions.

St. Annes-on-Sea:

The Fylde International Sand Yacht Club's "flying mile" races take place each week-end during September and October for the Corporation Trophy. The Sand Yacht Club is one of the few in Great Britain; the club house is on Clifton Drive North, St. Annes, and the races take place on the beach between St. Annes and Blackpool.

OCTOBER

Blackpool:
The Miners' Brass Band Contest has for its venue the Winter Gardens Pavilion, Blackpool, and lasts for one week.

Pendle Forest and Craven Hunt:
Meets are held in an area between Whalley and Skipton from October to March, on Tuesdays and Saturdays.

NOVEMBER

Bolton:
A two-day chrysanthemum show is held at the Town Hall during November.

Paythorne Bridge:
This bridge crosses the river Ribble in the Trough of Bowland. Crowds gather here on "Salmon Sunday", the Sunday nearest November 20th to watch for the arrival of the salmon.

MAPS:

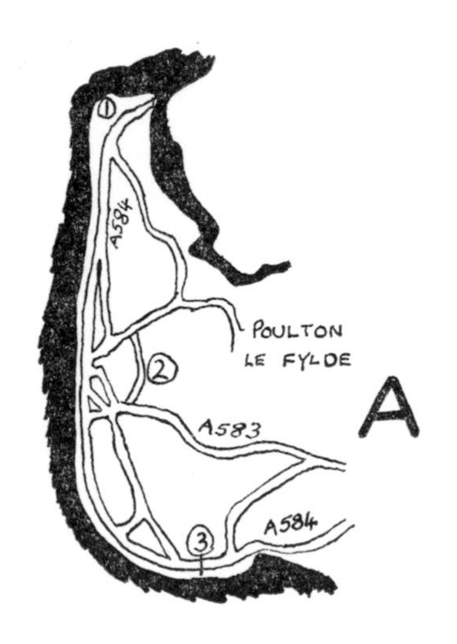
A584
POULTON
LE FYLDE
A583
A584
A

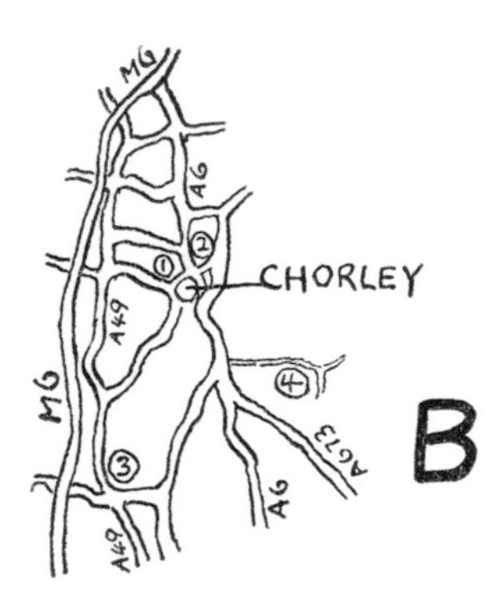
M6
A6
CHORLEY
A49
M6
A673
A6
A49
B

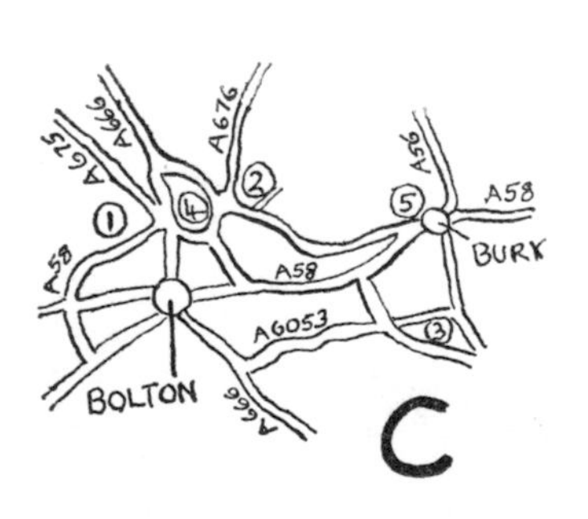
A675
A666
A676
A56
A58
A58
A58
BURY
A6053
BOLTON
A666
C

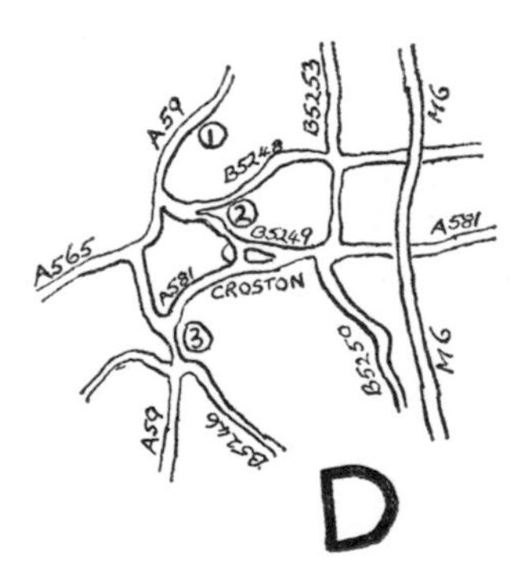
A59
B5253
M6
B5248
B5249
A581
A565
A581
CROSTON
B5250
M6
A59
B5246
D

Maps *(continued)*

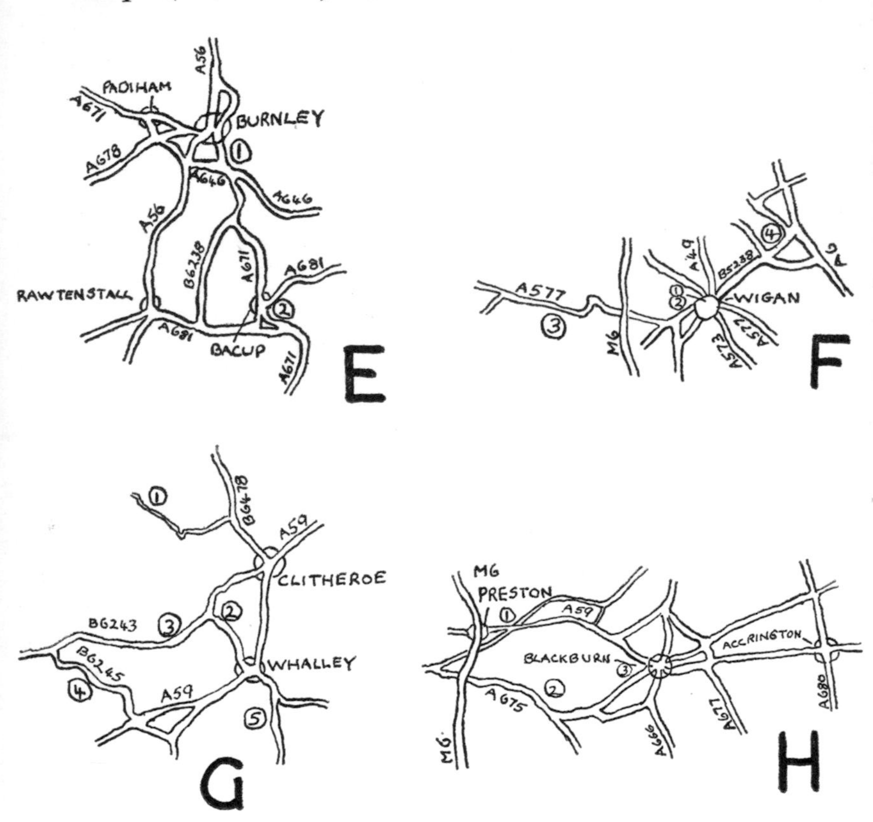

KEY TO MAPS:

A 1. Fleetwood
2. Blackpool Zoo
3. Lytham Museum

B 1. Astley Hall, Chorley
2. Chorley Church
3. Standish Church
4. Rivington Church

C 1. Smithills Hall, Bolton
2. Bradshaw Church
3. Radcliffe Church
4. Hall-i'-th'-Wood, Bolton
5. Bury Art Gallery

D 1. Hoole Church
2. Carr Howse, Bretherton
3. Rufford Old Hall

E 1. Townley Hall
2. Bacup Museum

F 1. Wigan Church
2. Art Gallery
3. Upholland
4. Haigh

G 1. Browsholme Hall
2. Great Mitton
3. Stoneyhurst
4. Ribchester
5. Great Harwood

H 1. Samlesbury Hall
2. Hoghton Tower
3. Blackburn Textile Museum

Index:

Index *(continued)*